Peter Shaw is a new writer for BRF in drama both in and outside the YMCA England, Peter has a Mast Goldsmiths College. He has had including a piece selected for the 2001 International Playwriting Festival at the Warehouse Theatre in Croydon, and a romantic comedy, *Love at First*, which toured in Surrey and West London in 2002, and was revived for the 2003 Edinburgh Fringe Festival.

Important information

Photocopying permission

The right to photocopy material in *All-age Sketches for the Christian Year* is granted for the pages that contain the photocopying clause: 'Reproduced with permission from *All-age Sketches for the Christian Year* published by BRF 2006 (1 84101 458 3)', so long as reproduction is for use in a teaching situation by the original purchaser. The right to photocopy material is not granted for anyone other than the original purchaser without written permission from BRF.

The Copyright Licensing Agency (CLA)

If you are resident in the UK and you have a photocopying licence with the Copyright Licensing Agency (CLA), please check the terms of your licence. If your photocopying request falls within the terms of your licence, you may proceed without seeking further permission. If your request exceeds the terms of your CLA licence, please contact the CLA directly with your request. Copyright Licensing Agency, 90 Tottenham Court Rd, London W1T 4LP. Tel 020 7631 5555; fax 020 7631 5500; email cla@cla.co.uk; web www.cla.co.uk. The CLA will provide photocopying authorization and royalty fee information on behalf of BRF.

BRF is a Registered Charity (No. 233280)

Text copyright © Peter Shaw 2006
The author asserts the moral right
to be identified as the author of this work

Published by
The Bible Reading Fellowship
First Floor, Elsfield Hall
15–17 Elsfield Way, Oxford OX2 8FG
Website: www.brf.org.uk

ISBN-10: 1 84101 458 3
ISBN-13: 978 1 84101 458 6
First published 2006
10 9 8 7 6 5 4 3 2 1 0
All rights reserved

Acknowledgments
Unless otherwise stated, scripture quotations are taken from the Contemporary
English Version of the Bible published by HarperCollins Publishers,
copyright © 1991, 1992, 1995 American Bible Society.

Performance and copyright
The right to perform *All-age Sketches for the Christian Year* drama material is
included in the purchase price, so long as the performance is in an amateur
context, for instance in church services, schools or holiday club venues. Where
any charge is made to audiences, written permission must be obtained from the
author, who can be contacted through the publishers. A fee or royalties may be
payable for the right to perform the script in that context.

A catalogue record for this book is available from the British Library

Printed in Singapore by Craft Print International Ltd

All-age Sketches

for the Christian Year

20 easy-to-perform sketches
for major festivals and popular celebrations

Peter Shaw

For my wonderful wife Sara,
a source of inspiration throughout the year

Contents

Foreword

Dramatic sketches are tricky things. They appear and are often criticized for being slight, one-dimensional, trivial and a form of propaganda. The humour, especially in some church circles, is often seen as irreverent or even blasphemous. Often the critics who hold these views miss the challenges that this form of drama presents. A good sketch will not tell you what to think but it may challenge your thinking. A good joke in a sketch may cause the sort of laughter that debunks prejudice and preconceptions.

This book has a wealth of short, accessible but challenging pieces for the whole year. Its satirical targets include justice (in 'One rotten apple'), sexism in the church ('One for the ladies'), and a biting attack on the treatment of the poor ('In for a penny') among many others. Audiences will enjoy the wit and imagination of these 20 mini-dramas but will also have some food for thought.

As well as satire, there are comic reworkings of Bible stories from unusual perspectives, offering fresh insights into faith. An interrogation room sets the scene for Pentecost in 'Gone with the wind', three camels chew over the significance of Epiphany ('Bearing gifts') and two stories of resurrection collide when Lazarus has trouble in a funeral parlour in 'Won't you roll away the stone?'

As Education Officer for Riding Lights Theatre Company, I work with professional actors and young people in their creation of entertaining and challenging theatre. I think this book presents performance opportunities for young and old alike, which, I am sure, will be of particular benefit to church youth and drama groups. The author's clear ideas for staging and production also make it accessible to those new to performance. This is an excellent drama resource.

Paul Birch, Riding Lights Theatre Company

Introduction

Welcome to this bumper book of drama sketches, which takes a journey through the Christian year, covering major festivals and events from Advent to Christ the King. Each of the short dramas is designed to be fun, fast and thought-provoking—taking a sideways look at each celebration and giving new insights and perspectives to age-old traditions.

These sketches are intended to complement rather than replace existing church ceremonies and customs and are flexible enough to be used on other occasions, at youth and outreach events, school camps, church weekends and entertainment evenings. Fun for all ages and suitable for a family audience, each sketch will delight children, won't embarrass teenagers, and will help adults to think about familiar events in a new way.

No more than four performers are required for each sketch, and many need just two. There are no elaborate costumes, sets, sound or special effects to arrange and the few props can be either found around the house or bought from a joke shop. Of course, this doesn't mean that the more adventurous performers can't go to town and organize a big show, with full sets, hired costumes, lights, sound, music...

In addition to the festivals of the Christian year, there are sketches for Father's Day and New Year, alongside popular events such as Christian Aid Week and the Week of Prayer for Christian Unity.

Traditional festivals such as Mothering Sunday, Corpus Christi, Candlemas and Christ the King are given new twists and fresh perspectives. So, if you've ever wondered what the wise men's camels discovered on their journey to Bethlehem, or what happened to Peter after he was arrested for being drunk and disorderly on the day of Pentecost, or how you can explain the Trinity using Jaffa Cakes, here's where you can find out.

The many celebrations at Christmas and Easter are covered in full, and each sketch has a brief introduction with tips on performing, sermon ideas, and relevant references from the Bible.

This book is all you need to bring these celebrations to life and inspire the church to think about such subjects as fatherhood, world poverty, who really is king of your life. The sketches provide a wonderful way to dramatize the Christian year, and when you've reached the end you can simply go back to the beginning and start all over again!

Notes on performing

I've kept the stage directions to a minimum so that you can adapt each piece to the place where you are performing, such as in church, a school hall, a tent or the open air. This also means that anyone with great ideas for how to stage the sketches won't feel restricted by intricate instructions.

There are three stage directions to denote a pause. BEAT indicates a short pause, THINKS is a short pause when a character is contemplating something, and PAUSE is a slightly longer break. The length of each one should be worked out in rehearsal but, as these are light-hearted, fast-paced dramas, don't linger too long.

After a speech/line of dialogue, there is sometimes a long dash '—' which indicates that the speech has been cut off, usually by another character interrupting. In these instances, it's a good idea to have in mind some additional words to say in case the next character fails to interrupt!

Alternatively, there may be three points '…' (ellipsis) at the end of a line. This indicates that the character speaking the lines has 'trailed off' mid-speech. If the following speech starts with another ellipsis, this indicates that the second character is continuing the speech from where the first character stopped.

Before you perform the pieces, my advice is to rehearse as much as possible and, if at all possible, learn the lines. The sketches are designed to be *performed*, not read, so you will need to use your face and eyes (not hidden behind a script) and your whole body, without having to grapple with page-turning halfway through a speech.

Once you have chosen the cast, have a read-through of the script a couple of times (sitting in a circle), then do it again a few times with actions. Mark up the script with notes on the actions and any dialogue alterations or cuts, then go away and learn the lines. Meet up again and have a few run-throughs without scripts and with props (with the director prompting). Shortly before the performance, try the sketch with costumes (a dress rehearsal) and lights/sound (a technical rehearsal) and one or two last times as if it is a performance (a final run-through with no stopping or prompting). Then it's the real thing!

Of course, many of these stages may not be possible or necessary, particularly if it's a small event. For example, you may like to use a sketch in a small group as an icebreaker: in this case, just bring along the scripts, give out characters to people who are happy to read, and have a bit of a laugh.

Thinking outside the box

Curtain up

Depending on the year, Advent Sunday falls either on the last Sunday in November or on the first Sunday in December. However, this sketch could be used in the weeks leading up to Advent Sunday, or at any time during Advent.

Bible backdrop

LUKE 1:26–33

Advent is all about expectation and excitement—a countdown to an earth-shattering event. We can imagine Mary's anxious last month leading up to the birth, after being told by an angel that her child '… will be great and will be called the Son of God Most High. The Lord God will make him king, as his ancestor David was. He will rule the people of Israel for ever, and his kingdom will never end.'

Sermon prompt

This sketch takes the idea of a countdown to the coming of Jesus as a baby from the perspective of a couple of chocolates in an Advent calendar. This approach should help children and adults to consider their Advent treats in a new way, and refocus the countdown to Christmas on the coming of Jesus.

It is no accident that the sketch shows the other trappings of Christmas—trees, presents, fairies, Father Christmas and so on—

being 'stripped away' as the chocolates are eaten, leaving only Jesus as a baby remaining. This could be used to open a discussion, or as the basis for a talk, about focusing on Jesus at Christmas time. But don't be too negative about the other things: chocolate and presents are good, too!

Cast

Two performers: CHOC 1 and CHOC 2 (both male or female). Although they are sweets, give them lots of character and emotion —they are in a very scary situation!

Staging: props, costumes and effects

This set-up requires two large cardboard boxes, each large enough to contain one of the two performers, situated side by side. The boxes are open at the front, so that the audience can see the performers. The back of each box is cut out and the gap covered with tinfoil.

The performers should be dressed in black (black trousers and tops) so as not to reveal their identity. Alternatively, they could be costumed as the chocolates they represent, an elf and a fairy—but obviously this will take more time and organization.

There are a couple of sound cues (footsteps), which can be either recorded and played at the appropriate time or 'performed' off stage by a third performer on a suitably noisy surface and into a microphone to enhance the dramatic effect.

Thinking outside the box

Scene: Two cardboard boxes on stage side by side, each with a tinfoil back. Inside the boxes are two figures: CHOC 1 and CHOC 2. They cannot see each other.

Choc 1: *(Whispering)* Hello? Hello? Anyone there? Hello? *(Listens to box containing CHOC 2)* Can anyone hear me?

Choc 2: *(Speaking through the side of the box)* Keep your voice down!

Choc 1: Thank goodness! I thought I was the last. *(Speaking through the side of the box)* Where are you?

Choc 2: Next box along. Do keep the noise down— they'll be coming soon.

Choc 1: Already? Another day gone?

Choc 2: *(Excited)* Not long now.

Choc 1: *(Concerned)* How many of us are left?

Choc 2: You and me. And the other one—

Choc 1: The last three. I remember when there were dozens of us.

Choc 2: 24, I've been counting. 21 gone. Only us left.

Choc 1: All of our friends. Gone. I remember them well. Robin—such a chirpy fellow.

Choc 2: … Good old Stocking. Full of surprises.

Reproduced with permission from *All-age Sketches for the Christian Year* published by BRF 2006 (1 84101 458 3)

www.barnabasinchurches.org.uk

Choc 1: And Snowman. One minute he was there, the next he'd disappeared.

Choc 2: Perhaps he melted.

Choc 1: No. It's always the same. First the footsteps. Loud, booming, thundering!

Choc 2: Then the voices. Always excited. *(Mimicking)* 'What will it be today?'

Choc 1: Then the creaking—like a great door being opened.

Choc 2: Sometimes it's deafening. Other times it seems further away.

Choc 1: But always followed by a metallic rustling sound.

Choc 2: … Tearing.

Choc 1: Then the voices again…

Choc 2: … Even more excited.

Choc 1: 'What is it?' they shout. Then we realize which of us it's got. Yesterday it was Mr Cracker…

Choc 2: … At least he went out with a bang.

Choc 1: But the novelty's worn off now. Whatever's happened to them… *(serious)* it'll be us soon. Next time they'll come for you or me, or the other one.

Choc 2: Exciting, isn't it? An adventure.

Choc 1: That's not what I'd call it.

Choc 2: It's what we've been waiting for—

Choc 1: Waiting? Or dreading…

Choc 2: But we don't know what it is…

Choc 1: Exactly. It's scary.

Choc 2: At least we know it's coming—

Choc 1: What's coming?

Choc 2: I don't know. But from the sound of the voices outside, it's terribly exciting. And we're part of it.

Choc 1: Part of what?

Choc 2: We'll find out. Maybe today, maybe tomorrow. And, if not then, definitely the day after that.

Choc 1: How'd you work that out?

Choc 2: Mathematics. There were 21 of us. But each day they've taken only one away. Only three of us left. So, in the next three days the mystery will be solved...

Choc 1: *(Resigned)* So that's it? In less than three days it'll all be over.

Choc 2: Or just beginning.

Choc 1: There must be a pattern here. Leading up to something—

Choc 2: There's a point to all this, that's for sure.

Choc 1: If only we had some clues.

Choc 2: Let's think what the other things are. The things that have gone.

Choc 1: There was Holly. Nice girl, if a little prickly.

Choc 2: There was that reindeer. Bit nosey, but all right once you'd given him a chance.

Choc 1: That big pudding's gone, too.

Reproduced with permission from *All-age Sketches for the Christian Year* published by BRF 2006 (1 84101 458 3)

www.barnabasinchurches.org.uk

Choc 2: So has Father Christmas.

Choc 1: Christmas! Of course. That's what it all has in common.

Choc 2: I've just realized, I've no idea what you are—

Choc 1: I've no idea what you are.

Choc 2: We might as well tell each other.

Choc 1: You're right. It may be a clue, and we are the last ones.

Choc 2: OK. I think—and this is just a guess—but I'm pretty sure I'm a fairy.

Choc 1: Gosh. That's quite impressive.

Choc 2: So what are you, then?

Choc 1: Um. An elf. One of Santa's helpers…

Choc 2: An elf and a fairy? Some help.

Choc 1: There must be a clue there. We just have to think outside the box…

Choc 2: Maybe there is no explanation.

Choc 1: There's a pattern to all this. It's building up to something… or someone. Didn't you say there was another one still here?

Choc 2: Yes. I heard someone.

Choc 1: What did they say?

Choc 2: It wasn't really talking. It was more like crying.

Choc 1: Maybe they're scared, too.

Choc 2: *(Getting excited)* No, it wasn't that sort of crying. It was like a baby.

Reproduced with permission from *All-age Sketches for the Christian Year* published by BRF 2006 (1 84101 458 3)
www.barnabasinchurches.org.uk

Choc 1: What's a baby doing here?

Choc 2: Maybe the baby is the answer—

Choc 1: *(Noise of footsteps)* Oh no! I can hear the footsteps.

Choc 2: Maybe all the things, the other things—crackers, presents, reindeer, trees, puddings, logs, Father Christmas…

Choc 1: What about you and me?

Choc 2: Yes! Even us—elves, fairies… Maybe we're all being stripped away—

Choc 1: *(Sound of footsteps getting louder)* They're getting closer. Why are we all being 'stripped away'?

Choc 2: So that it just leaves the most important thing until last—

Choc 1: A baby? But—

Choc 2: Shush! They're coming. I wonder which of us it will be…?

CHOC 2 suddenly bursts out through the tinfoil at the back of the box. Sounds of excitement are heard off stage. Then the sounds die down. CHOC 1 is alone.

Choc 1: Hello? Hello? Is anyone there? *(Pause as CHOC 1 listens)* Oh no! The fairy has gone now! I've still no idea what's happening. And I've a horrible feeling… This time tomorrow, it'll be me!

* * * END * * *

Who's been sleeping in my manger?

Curtain up

This is a fun, fast sketch designed to fit into the usually packed-to-bursting Christmas carol service, leaving lots of time for carols and the traditional nativity play. It is also simple enough to be performed at a service on Christmas morning. If you are performing the sketch on Christmas Day, remember: there are less than 365 shopping days to go!

Bible backdrop

LUKE 2:1–20

The nativity, the story of Jesus' birth, is about incarnation, not inconvenience. However, Emperor Augustus' order for a census to be carried out must have seemed ill-timed and greatly inconvenient to Mary and Joseph. The decree from far-away Rome must have caused a scurry of activity in distant Judea, but no one could have realized the divine significance of its timing as the young couple set out on their journey from Nazareth to Bethlehem.

Sermon prompt

'Christmas has got too commercial,' people often cry—to which the usual reply is, 'Tell us something we don't know!' It's easy to get cynical about all the trappings of Christmas—the expense and the excess—but we need to make sure that in all the festivities we don't miss out on the most important thing, the birth of Jesus. We also, as Christians, don't want to raise so many objections to the excesses of Christmas that we throw the baby out with the baubles.

The message of the sketch is clear, but, because it doesn't explain the significance of Jesus, it would be best to pair it with a talk or presentation that does.

Cast

Three performers are needed: DADDY OX (male), MUMMY OX (female) and BABY OX (male or female).

Staging: props, costumes and effects

Either find some oxen or brown cow costumes or kit the actors out with brown T-shirts and a few bits and bobs like horns, udders or a tail—so long as it gives an overall impression. You can use the same set of costumes if you have a nativity play, and the only props you need are three blankets.

Who's been sleeping in my manger?

Scene: A cattle shed in Bethlehem (with an overbooked inn next door), home to three oxen: DADDY OX, MUMMY OX and BABY OX. MUMMY OX and BABY OX are seated on stage. DADDY OX enters. He is cross.

Daddy: That's it. I've had it up to here. I can't take any more. Call the family to order!

Mummy: *(Jumps up, shouts)* All oxen fall in! *(Pause, clears throat)* On the double!

Baby: *(Gets up)* Oh, very well. *(Comes over and lines up next to Mummy Ox)*

Mummy: Oxen standing by. *(Salutes)*

Daddy: Well done, Mummy Ox.

Mummy: Thanks, Daddy Ox.

Daddy: We all know what day it is tomorrow? (BEAT) Baby Ox?

Baby: Census day.

Mummy: Ooh! I'm *so* excited—

Daddy: Quiet! I'm sorry to say I'm *not* excited. In fact, I'm fed up to the back teeth. Everyone's gone mad! Decorations, cards, presents. Lunacy!

Mummy: But census time is special. Everyone gathered together, distant relations you haven't seen for ages...

www.barnabasinchurches.org.uk

Daddy: Huh! Stuck indoors all day with your mad cow of an auntie? We'll all get stuffed with food, play some games till we all get bored. Then the arguments start. Not this year. We're going away.

Mummy: We can't go away on census day!

Baby: Where's your census spirit?

Daddy: It wore out when they started the countdown. 'Only 106 shopping days to go!' Not for us. There will be no census day. Grab your blankets—we're going out into the fields to get away from it all.

MUMMY OX and BABY OX go to fetch their blankets.

Mummy: Sorry, love. But you know what he's like.

Baby: Yes. I do think he's right in some ways. But I have a strange feeling that if we go away we might miss out on something special...

Mummy: I think his mind's made up.

They grab their blankets and move over to DADDY OX.

Daddy: Let's go somewhere on earth where we can get some peace. Goodbye, lowly cattle shed. Shut the door on the way out please, Ox junior.

They exit. BABY OX shuts the door. Time passes. They return, a few days later. MUMMY and DADDY enter with blankets wrapped around themselves. BABY has no blanket.

Reproduced with permission from *All-age Sketches for the Christian Year* published by BRF 2006 (1 84101 458 3)

www.barnabasinchurches.org.uk

Daddy: I thought I told you to shut the door! Were you born in a barn?

Baby: I'm an ox, so of course I was!

Daddy: *(To MUMMY)* How rude! Did you hear that?

Mummy: Well, you haven't given us a moment's peace since we left!

Daddy: After all I've done to give you a stable home to live in, a stable environment to grow up in, a stable... (THINKS) stable.

Baby: I'm freezing.

Daddy: That'll teach you to give your blanket away.

Baby: *(Looking around)* I'm sure I shut that door when I left.

Mummy: Some holiday. Tempest, storm and wind! I feel like I haven't slept in a week.

Daddy: What were those shepherds shouting at by night?

Mummy: I don't know. I hid under my blanket after the light show began.

Daddy: Then they started the karaoke! What were those strange visitors singing? I'll give them 'peace on earth'! How about goodwill to oxen who are trying get a good night's kip? Not exactly the restful break I hoped it would be.

Baby: Someone's been in here!

Mummy: It wasn't that bad. We did meet that nice little donkey on the dusty road.

Reproduced with permission from *All-age Sketches for the Christian Year* published by BRF 2006 (1 84101 458 3)
www.barnabasinchurches.org.uk

Daddy: Sounded like he was having a worse census time than us. Carrying that young woman and her unborn baby for miles to Bethlehem. They hadn't even made a booking! There'll be no room at the inn, I said... not on census day!

Baby: Come over here and look! *(Points at straw)*

Daddy: Hang on! Someone's been sleeping in my straw!

Mummy: *(Comes over)* And someone's been sleeping in my straw!

Baby: *(Comes over)* And someone's been sleeping in my manger!

Daddy: And they're still there! (BEAT) No, hang on a sec—it's just a blanket. *(Examines blanket)*

Baby: That's my blanket!

Daddy: I thought you gave it to the donkey—for when the baby was born.

Baby: They must have stayed here. The young couple with the donkey, they must have had their baby here!

Daddy: Yes... those strange people who sang to the shepherds, they said something about a baby. But they said he was a king.

Mummy: A king! Born here? Not in this poor lowly stable!

Baby: Hmm. Daddy Ox, you were so anxious to get away from all the festivities that we've missed out on a wonderful thing. A new king was

Reproduced with permission from *All-age Sketches for the Christian Year* published by BRF 2006 (1 84101 458 3)
www.barnabasinchurches.org.uk

born. And we could have welcomed him in, joined the celebrations. Now we've missed it all!

* * * END * * *

24

Should auld acquaintance be forgot?

Curtain up

Ideally, this sketch should be performed as close to New Year's Day as possible, but the first week back after the New Year celebrations will be fine if you can't manage 31 December or 1 January.

Bible backdrop

PHILIPPIANS 4:13

This verse says, 'Christ gives me strength to face anything'. Paul was in prison when he wrote this letter to the Philippians, but his lack of freedom did not prevent him from sharing the gospel with all who came to him. Satisfied with whatever he has, his words are an inspiration to us as we approach the new year.

Sermon prompt

New Year, while not a traditional church festival, is widely celebrated both inside and outside the church. It is a time when we take stock of the year, have a bit of a party, and use the opportunity to make a fresh start.

While these are all good things, we sometimes feel pressurized to make big changes: give up smoking or chocolate, go to the gym or start a strict new diet. Christians often resolve to pray more, read the Bible more or worship more—and usually we set ourselves huge, unattainable challenges that make us feel a failure come February.

This sketch simply points out that this can be unhelpful and that we can't change our lives through our own strength and determination. We should seek God for the small steps to change our lives and deepen our relationship with him—and ask for his help to make it possible.

Cast

Two performers: ONE and TWO (male or female). One wants to do what's right but finds it hard going; the other seems to be able to change and be more holy in his or her own strength.

Staging: props, costumes and effects

ONE and TWO are having a New Year celebration, so should be covered in streamers and wear novelty hats and so on. There are a few scene changes (to denote the passing of each year) but these should be almost instantaneous. There are no props required apart from some party poppers, party blowers and a couple of glasses for the toast.

Should auld acquaintance be forgot?

Scene: A New Year party. ONE and TWO are counting in the New Year.

One & Two: *(Looking at watches)* Ten, nine, eight, seven, six, five, four, three, two, one… *(They hug, dance around and then start singing)* Should auld acquaintance be forgot and never brought to mind? (THINK) La, la, la, la-la, la, la, la… For auld lang syne, my dear, for auld lang syne… (THINK) La, la, la, la-la, la, la, la… for auld lang syne.

One: Good old Lang Syne. Old Lang Syne. Who was Lang Syne, anyway?

Two: He was an old friend—more of an acquaintance, really—of Robert Burns. But he only saw him once a year. All their mutual friends used to gather at 'old' Lang's house on the 31st of December for a get-together. It became a bit of a tradition. Burns wrote a song about it and… you know. The rest is history.

One: Is that true?

Two: Apparently.

One: *(Raises glass)* Thanks, Burnsey and Syney, for a good auld celebration.

Two: Well, I can't stick around here—it's the New Year and there's resolutions to fulfil, you know.

Reproduced with permission from *All-age Sketches for the Christian Year* published by BRF 2006 (1 84101 458 3)

www.barnabasinchurches.org.uk

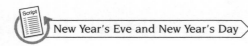

One: I totally forgot about resolutions this year. What's yours?

Two: I was thinking—prayer is very important.

One: Oh, essential.

Two: And I don't think that I pray enough.

One: You certainly can't do too much—

Two: Ah. But you can do too little.

One: True.

Two: That's why this year, starting now, I've committed to pray regularly—

One: Good on you.

Two: Every day, in fact—

One: At the very least.

Two: Without exception—

One: Me too!

Two: For a whole hour.

One: *(Slightly taken aback)* An hour, you say?

Two: 60 minutes. Oh, yes.

One: I'm sure that's a very, um… spiritual… course of action.

Two: Just imagine it. 365 hours of prayer in a year. Think what a difference it will make— Are you with me?

One: Absolutely. One hour—

Two: *(Determined)* Every. Single. Day.

One: Right.

Reproduced with permission from *All-age Sketches for the Christian Year* published by BRF 2006 (1 84101 458 3)
www.barnabasinchurches.org.uk

Two: It's agreed. I'll meet you back here in just under a year's time to see how we've fared.

One: See you next year. Happy... praying.

They both leave and return seconds later.

One & Two: *(Greet each other)* Hello!

One: So, did you have a good... year?

Two: Average to middling. How was your prayer time?

One: The resolution?

Two: To commit to praying—

One: Every day—

Two: For an hour.

One: Yes. Good. (BEAT) Well, it started off really good. Very nearly an hour on day one. Day two was more tricky—

Two: Oh?

One: But I managed a good 50 minutes or so. The thing is, I didn't always... not every day, that is... and not always for a whole hour. And by February, well, late January actually... things started to tail off a little. It was a bit... ambitious. Don't you think? How did you get along?

Two: Yes, I struggled—

One: *(Breathes a sigh of relief)* You're only human—

Two: I struggled to keep to just an hour. Most days I overran...

Reproduced with permission from *All-age Sketches for the Christian Year* published by BRF 2006 (1 84101 458 3)

www.barnabasinchurches.org.uk

One: Gosh, you make me feel a bit… awful. I sometimes think these resolutions were thought up to make people feel guilty—

Two: Actually, the idea of a New Year resolution was invented by a Roman emperor in AD682.

One: Oh yeah? Which one?

Two: Emperor (BEAT) Terry.

One: Emperor Terry?

Two: The third. Terry III had a very bad year in AD681—lost his keys, fell down a manhole, accidentally invaded the Isle of Wight, that sort of thing. So he decided to make up for it in 682. Hence he invented New Year resolutions.

One: Is that true?

Two: Apparently.

One: *(Looks at watch)* Oh. Gosh, it's nearly that time again, only a minute to go. Bit late for another resolution—

Two: I already have one. I've decided to read the Bible more—

One: More, as in…?

Two: Every day.

One: What, for an hour?

Two: Yes.

One: Well, I suppose, if you managed it last time with prayer…

Reproduced with permission from *All-age Sketches for the Christian Year* published by BRF 2006 (1 84101 458 3)
www.barnabasinchurches.org.uk

Two: ... On top of my hour of prayer.

One: One hour of prayer and an hour of Bible study? Two hours a day—?

Two: Are you joining me?

One: I think it's a good idea, but—

Two: Not important to you, is it, the Bible?

One: Of course, I think it would be invaluable—

Two: That's settled, then. *(Looks at watch)* Five, four...

One & Two: Three, two, one... *(They hug, dance around and then start singing)* Should auld acquaintance be forgot... (THINK) La, la, la, la-la, la! La, la, la, la-la, la, la, la... (THINK) For auld lang syne...

Two: Best be getting off if we want to fulfil our resolutions.

One: See you back here in a year.

Two: Good luck!

One: *(To himself)* I'll need it.

They both leave and return seconds later.

One & Two: *(Greet each other)* Hello!

One: So, did you have a good... another year?

Two: OK to reasonable. How was your resolution? To pray and read the Bible every day? (BEAT) Two hours a day?

One: *(Avoiding the question)* How was it for you?

Two: Not good.

One: Didn't quite make it?

Two: May the 17th. Nightmare!

One: Missed that day, did you? It's always hard to keep going when—

Two: Bedridden. Struck down with insomnia, narcolepsy, you name it! Checked the old watch, thought I'd missed a day out! But, thank heavens, through my feverish haze I'd misread it! Did the two hours with 20 minutes to go! *(Wipes brow)* Phew-we! Yourself?

One: Better than last year.

Two: You managed it?

One: No. Failed. March the 12th. After twelve hours on a bouncy castle, fell asleep during Lamentations. Don't ask. Went a bit pear-shaped after that.

Two: You know what they say about falling off a horse?

One: Next time take a taxi?

Two: Get right back on, or you'll never ride again. Gosh, it's nearly another New Year…

One: That's right. (THINKS) You know what always puzzles me about New Year? Why is December the 25th not New Year's Day? In the year minus one BC, they changed from BC to AD seven days after the birth of Jesus. So, that means Jesus spent his first week 'before Christ'. What's that all about?

Reproduced with permission from *All-age Sketches for the Christian Year* published by BRF 2006 (1 84101 458 3)
www.barnabasinchurches.org.uk

Two: Emperor Terry III again. You know how the queen has two birthdays?

One: Actual and official?

Two: Right. Terry reckoned so should Jesus. 25th of December the real one, first of January 'official'.

One: So when did it become New Year?

Two: That's thanks to Robbie Burns and Auld Lang Syne. They thought it was confusing and felt that the change of calendar needed its own celebration. So they called it 'Renewing the Yearling'. Eventually shortened to New Year.

One: Is that true?

Two: Apparently. So, are you joining me for the next challenge? Worship!

One: For an hour a day?

Two: As well as—

One: Praying and reading the Bible.

Two: Those things not important to you?

One: Yes, of course—

Two: Good. *(Looks at watch)* Nearly there... five, four...

One & Two: *(ONE a little weary)* ... three, two, one... *(They hug and then start singing)* Should auld acquaintance... (THINK) La, la-la, la, la, la, la, la, la, la!

Two: Must dash. Happy praying, Bible reading and worshipping! Only one thousand and ninety-five hours to fill!

Reproduced with permission from *All-age Sketches for the Christian Year* published by BRF 2006 (1 84101 458 3)

www.barnabasinchurches.org.uk

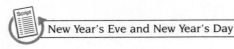

One: Yes. *(Weary)* See you back here—

Two: In a year!

They leave and return seconds later.

Two: *(Greeting ONE)* Hello!

One: Hi. And before you ask. No. Failed. Miserably. Day three. Nervous exhaustion.

Two: It was tough, I'll admit.

One: But you managed it?

Two: Yes. Success once again. In the words of the great Terry III—

One: I've been thinking. Praying, actually. And listening, more to the point. Now, this year's resolution—

Two: Fasting?

One: No. I'm giving up something. A number of things, actually. Like... making impossible resolutions. And breaking impossible resolutions.

Two: You're giving up?

One: Yes. I'm giving up rules, and taking up relationship. I'll spend time praying, reading the Bible, worshipping, fasting... spending time with God. All those things. But because I want to, not because I'm supposed to.

Two: Oh. (PAUSE) In that case, I might have to join you in your 'giving up'.

Reproduced with permission from *All-age Sketches for the Christian Year* published by BRF 2006 (1 84101 458 3)
www.barnabasinchurches.org.uk

One: What have you got to give up that's bad? I'd be surprised if you have enough hours in the day...

Two: I'm giving up... um... (BEAT) Lying.

One: I didn't think you had time to sleep...

Two: No, not lying down. Making things up. Not telling the truth.

One: What like?

Two: Oh, you know, all that stuff about Old Lang Syne and Robbie Burns. And Emperor Terry. The third.

One: They were all lies?

Two: Yes. And there was something else you're really not going to like. All that stuff about praying. And reading the Bible. And worshipping. Every day. For an hour.

One: (*Angry*) You don't mean?

Two: (*Backing away*) 'Fraid so. All made up. Couldn't admit that I'd failed miserably too.

One: Well, well. So no more impossible resolutions, eh? Just manageable adjustments...

Two: ... One step at a time. Yeah!

One: See you back here then—

Two: In a year!

They shake hands and exit.

* * * END * * *

Reproduced with permission from *All-age Sketches for the Christian Year* published by BRF 2006 (1 84101 458 3)

www.barnabasinchurches.org.uk

Bearing gifts

Curtain up

Epiphany falls on 6 January, so the festival is celebrated on the nearest Sunday, usually the third Sunday after Christmas.

Bible backdrop

MATTHEW 2:1–12

Epiphany, which means 'manifestation', celebrates the coming of the magi (also called wise men or kings) to visit Jesus shortly after his birth. It is the first time Jesus is 'shown' to people who are not of the Jewish faith.

Sermon prompt

This sketch is set shortly before Epiphany and is from the perspective of the magi's camels en route to Bethlehem. They are unaware of the purpose of the journey and must glean an impression of the person they are visiting from the gifts they are carrying—gold, frankincense and myrrh.

The sketch is a simple way to reflect on the three aspects of Jesus' life that these gifts reveal: his kingship, his priesthood, and his death. It is also distinguished in that it is probably the only comedy sketch ever written about Epiphany that doesn't contain a frankincense–Frankenstein joke.

Cast

Three performers: QUASIMODO, HUMPHREY and FRANK (all male or female). The characters are three rather exhausted camels.

Staging: props, costumes and effects

Props are required for the gold, frankincense and myrrh, which you may already have from your nativity play. If not, make some in the usual fashion using decorated cardboard boxes and so on. Lots of fun can be had making costumes for the camels, but they could simply be given large rucksacks to wear (the sketch makes it clear from the outset that they are camels).

Bearing gifts

Scene: In the desert at night, three camels—QUASIMODO, HUMPHREY and FRANK—lie down to rest. Their masters are away.

Quasimodo: I tell you what. I've got the hump.

Humphrey: We're camels, Quasimodo. We're supposed to.

Quasimodo: I don't mean that, Humphrey. I'm annoyed. Where are we, anyway?

Frank: No idea.

Humphrey: I'm lost too.

Quasimodo: We three camels disoriented are.

Frank: How far have we come?

Humphrey: We've traversed afar. We've been on the road for ages. What's the date, Frank?

Frank: I dunno. Can't get used to this new calendar. It's been a long journey.

Quasimodo: First we crossed that field…

Frank: … came to a fountain…

Humphrey: … over the moor…

Quasimodo: … then a mountain…

Frank: … following yonder star…

Humphrey: Oh. Oh. (BEAT) Is that what it is? Seems more like a comet to me.

Reproduced with permission from *All-age Sketches for the Christian Year* published by BRF 2006 (1 84101 458 3)
www.barnabasinchurches.org.uk

Quasimodo: From where I am—tied to the back of you, Frank—it looks like Uranus.

Frank: I tell you it's a star, Quasimodo. Pretty unusual one by all accounts. Moving about in the heavens.

Quasimodo: Thank goodness it's stopped for a bit so we can rest.

Humphrey: What are we following it for, Frank?

Frank: The masters want to, Humphrey. They're astronomers.

Quasimodo: Yeah, astronomers. So it's not like they've got a hectic social life. A star shooting about in the sky's probably the most exciting thing that's ever happened to them.

Frank: I've got a hunch—if you'll pardon the expression—that there's more to this journey than meets the eye.

Quasimodo: They certainly packed a lot of stuff for the trip. Telescopes, astral charts, anoraks…

Humphrey: And it must be a pretty important journey. Before we set off, they spent hours ironing their underpants.

Frank: I told you, they're astronomers. They do that every day. But there's definitely something different about this trip. They even polished their camel clips.

Humphrey: And remember those mysterious parcels they spent ages wrapping.

Reproduced with permission from *All-age Sketches for the Christian Year* published by BRF 2006 (1 84101 458 3)
www.barnabasinchurches.org.uk

Quasimodo: Yeah, on top of all that other junk. When they loaded mine on, it was the last straw! I thought it was going to break me back! (BEAT) Why is it always us camels who have to lump stuff over the desert? Couldn't they have found another way of shipping it about?

Humphrey: Such as?

Quasimodo: One could have gone in a taxi, one in a car, one on a scooter beeping his hooter—

Humphrey: Quasimodo? Have you got sunstroke?

Frank: *(Thinking)* But it's those strange parcels that puzzle me…

Humphrey: What about them, Frank?

Frank: I'm sure they are the key to this journey, Humphrey. Perhaps they're gifts!

Humphrey: Who for?

Frank: For whoever we're journeying to see. Must be someone very special.

Humphrey: Who's important to a group of astronomers?

Quasimodo: Someone who's stolen their telescope?

Frank: An important person, yes. A very important person. The most important person.

Quasimodo: Patrick Moore?

Humphrey: Whoever it is, I don't suppose we'll find out until we get there.

Reproduced with permission from *All-age Sketches for the Christian Year* published by BRF 2006 (1 84101 458 3)
www.barnabasinchurches.org.uk

Quasimodo: Where's there? It could be miles away. I don't think I'll make it with all this junk on my back. Look at that mountain up ahead. It'd be easier going through the eye of a needle...

Humphrey: If we knew who this 'important person' was, that would make the journey easier. Give us a purpose.

Frank: Why don't we take a peek at those presents? Maybe they'll give us a clue.

Quasimodo: But Frank, what if they catch us?

Humphrey: They've gone off to have a rest, drink a flask of tea, smoke a few cigars. They won't be back for ages.

Frank: Come on. Let's start with yours, Quasimodo. (*Rummages in QUASIMODO's pack; finds something*) Here it is! (*Shows Gift 1*)

Quasimodo: What is it? (*Takes and unwraps Gift 1*) It's awfully heavy...

Humphrey: (*Takes Gift 1*) It's a great big lump of gold. Very ornate. Worth a tidy sum, I reckon.

Quasimodo: Do you think the person we're going to see is poor?

Frank: (*Takes Gift 1 back*) Or rich. This is more like the sort of thing you'd take to a king. To impress him.

Humphrey: So it must be someone important. Well, we knew that. What's in my parcel?

Reproduced with permission from *All-age Sketches for the Christian Year* published by BRF 2006 (1 84101 458 3)
www.barnabasinchurches.org.uk

Frank: *(Opening HUMPHREY's pack)* I dunno, but it smells a bit—

Quasimodo: Is that what it is? I thought it was that curry we had in Syria.

Frank: No, this is a different smell. Sweet, like the sap of a plant—

Humphrey: I've smelt it before somewhere. Haven't you, Frank?

Frank: Yes. Outside a temple—

Humphrey: I've got it. I know what it is, Frank—incense!

Frank: Of course!

Humphrey: But not just any incense, Frank. It's frankincense. *(Unwraps and reveals Gift 2)*

Quasimodo: *(Takes Gift 2)* Isn't that what priests use?

Frank: That's right. *(Takes Gift 2)* Must be for a holy man.

Humphrey: But that doesn't tie up. How can this person be a priest and a king? Aren't priests supposed to live modestly?

Frank: The plot thickens. Open my pack. Maybe that'll shed more light on the subject.

Quasimodo: *(Opening FRANK's pack)* Yours is a bit whiffy, too. *(Produces and unwraps Gift 3)*

Humphrey: *(Takes Gift 3)* I've smelt this before as well.

Quasimodo: I pulled a cart for some undertakers a few years ago. That's what the bodies smelt like. *(Takes Gift 3)* It's some sort of balm.

Reproduced with permission from *All-age Sketches for the Christian Year* published by BRF 2006 (1 84101 458 3)
www.barnabasinchurches.org.uk

Humphrey: *(Excited)* Myrrh. Myrrh! Myrrh!

Frank: Have you got a chill?

Humphrey: No, that's what they call it, myrrh. And Quasimodo's right. They sprinkle it over the bandages they wrap round people who have died.

Frank: Yuck! No wonder people have been giving me a wide berth.

Quasimodo: Do you think this person we're off to see is going to die?

Frank: Then why bring the other presents? A king, a priest... and now this?

Humphrey: What does it mean?

Quasimodo: It means we're no closer to finding out who this star-attracting person is—

Frank: Talking of the star, look up there!

Humphrey: It's on the move! Westward leading—

Frank: Still proceeding—

Quasimodo: And the masters are coming back. That means we're off again. Why is life such a constant burden, Frank?

Frank: Well, I suppose that's the problem with being a camel. Wherever you are. And wherever you go...

ALL: You've always got the hump.

* * * END * * *

Reproduced with permission from *All-age Sketches for the Christian Year* published by BRF 2006 (1 84101 458 3)

www.barnabasinchurches.org.uk

When two or more

Curtain up

The Week of Prayer for Christian Unity always falls from 18 to 25 January, regardless of the days of the week.

Bible backdrop

PSALM 133:1; ROMANS 15:5; JOHN 17:20–21

Throughout the Bible, there are many calls for us to live in unity with each other and with God. Primarily, the call for unity is about Jesus' own prayer in John 17: 'I want all of them to be one with each other, just as I am one with you and you are one with me.' Ultimately, Jesus' reason for this prayer is so that 'the people of this world will believe that you sent me'. There is no greater reason than this for Christians to be in unity with each other.

Sermon prompt

The Week of Prayer for Christian Unity is a time for Christians from different denominations, traditions, places and backgrounds to come together in prayer to celebrate and strengthen the bond that we all share in Christ. However, it is easy to fall into the trap of thinking that *our* church has the right emphasis on freedom and reverence, law and grace, tolerance and intolerance and it is the church down the road that has it wrong.

Praying for unity is not about trying to change others to be more like us, or for us to try to be more like others. It is an opportunity to celebrate differences, embrace diversity and recognize that God can meet us where we are, whatever expression of Christianity we adopt.

This sketch needs to be performed sensitively, as its message is mostly the opposite of what is expressed by the characters. It would be advisable to contextualize the sketch and use it as an opportunity to open a discussion about unity.

Cast

Two performers: MAN and WOMAN, representing two 'ordinary' churchgoers.

Staging: props, costumes and effects

A very simple set-up, with everyday clothing, a sofa if possible (or two or three chairs covered with cloth to look like a sofa). Props include a tray of biscuits and teacups to clear away.

When two or more

Scene: A living room where a meeting has taken place. MAN has just shown the last two visitors out.

Man: *(Shutting the door)* Well, that was... interesting.

Woman: *(MAN joins WOMAN on the sofa)* Thank goodness. I thought we'd never get that last couple out the door. They were harder to get rid of than black pudding at a vegan garden party.

Man: The rest of them couldn't leave fast enough. I think those two scared them off.

Woman: Can you blame them? They had some quite extreme views.

Man: Extreme? They made Genghis Khan look like Mother Teresa. And they didn't mind sharing their opinions.

Woman: They certainly weren't putting the 'fun' in fundamentalist.

Man: No. They were doing their best to put the 'mentalist' in fundamentalist. It really put a damper on the evening when they piped up at the end. But there was no stopping them...

Woman: Oh, they were harmless, really...

Man: You weren't listening when they were rattling off a list of programmes they'd complained about to the Broadcasting Standards Commission.

Reproduced with permission from *All-age Sketches for the Christian Year* published by BRF 2006 (1 84101 458 3)
www.barnabasinchurches.org.uk

Woman: *(Picks up tray of biscuits)* At least they do something about it. We're always sat here moaning—but we've never managed to put pen to paper. *(Takes tray out)*

Man: I'm glad about that now. I don't want to be bracketed with those cranks.

Woman: *(Returns. Sits on sofa)* That's a bit harsh.

Man: Their list of programmes that are 'destroying the moral fibre of this country' included *Bob the Builder*, *Ant and Dec's Saturday Night Takeaway*, and *Last of the Summer Wine*! I think they must go to bed at eight o'clock every evening before the proper degrading filth is broadcast.

Woman: *(Firm but friendly)* You're doing it again. Stop it.

Man: OK—I know. Let's look at the positive things. (BEAT) It was a good turn-out.

Woman: Yes. And lots of representatives from different places. Good age range.

Man: People prayed a lot. This is, to say the least, important for a prayer meeting.

Woman: Yeah—I thought that woman in the stripy top was never going to stop.

Man: She must be on a diet of Lucozade and black coffee. One of them rambled on for about twelve minutes. I started timing it in the end.

Woman: *(Shaking her head)* You didn't!

Reproduced with permission from *All-age Sketches for the Christian Year* published by BRF 2006 (1 84101 458 3)
www.barnabasinchurches.org.uk

Man: What else was I supposed to do? I couldn't follow what she was saying! Something about this area being like a giant shoe?

Woman: Oh yeah. She knew an awful lot about shoes from the evidence of that prayer.

Man: Maybe she works in a shoe shop—she was certainly talking cobblers. What was it she said? The church is the tongue of the shoe but it's tied up by the laces…?

Woman: What were the laces? Did she say the Borough Council?

Man: No, that was the heel. I think the laces were local kids with ASBOs.

Woman: But that doesn't make any sense—didn't she say they had to be untied?

Man: Don't ask me. I was long gone by then.

Woman: What was supposed to be represented by the sole?

Man: Pedestrianization of the town centre. Shall we just conclude that she didn't really think through the extended shoe metaphor, before foisting it on all of us for nearly 13 minutes?

Woman: She was something else. Then there was that man who kept praying about Switzerland. *(Frowning)* What was that all about?

Man: That was brilliant, though. Whatever people prayed about—the government, healing, even that strange prayer about the lack of milk

Reproduced with permission from *All-age Sketches for the Christian Year* published by BRF 2006 (1 84101 458 3)
www.barnabasinchurches.org.uk

delivery rounds—he always managed to bring it back to Switzerland. *(Giggling)* I nearly died when he said he had a prophetic picture for that old bloke with the red nose.

Woman: *(Quoting)* 'I can see some sort of clock… It's a cuckoo clock…'

MAN and WOMAN crack up.

Man: Maybe he works for the Swiss Tourist Board.

Woman: But the best thing was when that plump girl got up and did a 'prophetic dance'. *(Gets up and demonstrates)*

Man: I had to bite my lip. I think the Swiss man thought she was having a fit—I don't think he'd seen anything like it before. He looked like he was about to lay hands on her and cast out demons…

Woman: We're doing it again. We said we wouldn't.

Man: But come on, it was a bit weird tonight.

Woman: Yes, but we're all different. We shouldn't be criticizing them—it's hardly in the spirit of the thing.

Man: I'm not criticizing. Some of it was pretty funny.

Woman: Unfortunately, not all of it. You were in the kitchen when the girl with the dreadlocks started arguing with the red-nosed man about animal rights.

Reproduced with permission from *All-age Sketches for the Christian Year* published by BRF 2006 (1 84101 458 3)

www.barnabasinchurches.org.uk

Man: How did that come up?

Woman: I've no idea. But anyway, I tried to make light of it—to no avail. She just wouldn't drop it. Didn't you notice the tension in the room when you came back with the teas?

Man: There's always tension. It's like that every time. People are used to their ways of doing things. When you gather so many different people in one place, it's bound to throw up a lot of issues.

Woman: It's an attitude thing. People should just bite their tongues for an hour. Or learn to accept people's differences. (BEAT) Mind you, we're not setting a very good example.

Man: I'm sure they're all doing the same now. Some of them probably found us a bit weird too.

Woman: At least we've done our turn now.

Man: Next time it's someone else's responsibility to host the infamous Week of Prayer for Christian Unity.

Woman: Yes. Thank God it only happens once a year.

* * * END * * *

Reproduced with permission from *All-age Sketches for the Christian Year* published by BRF 2006 (1 84101 458 3)
www.barnabasinchurches.org.uk

Candles in the bin

Curtain up

Candlemas falls on 2 February. This date is six weeks after Christmas, midway between the shortest day and the spring equinox.

Bible backdrop

LUKE 2:22–40; JOHN 8:12; MATTHEW 5:14–16; LUKE 11:33

Candlemas is a celebration of the time when Jesus, just six weeks old, was taken to the temple by Mary and Joseph as a thanksgiving to God for his birth. Christians mark this time with a festival of light, when churches are lit up with multiple candles, reminding us that Jesus is the light for the world. But it doesn't stop there, as, in Matthew's Gospel, Jesus tells us that we Christians are also the light for the world.

Sermon prompt

It is often the case that Christians, as they lose sight of the excitement of their first encounter with Jesus, let their light grow dimmer and lose their enthusiasm to minister and share their light with other people.

This sketch is about someone who has hidden his or her light for a long time—so long, in fact, that he or she no longer even understands why other people would find it attractive. It could be used to challenge people about how they have hidden their light, and lead to a time of ministry to pray for them to let their light shine out once more. The sketch could also be used shortly before a mission or outreach event to excite people about sharing their faith and light with others.

Cast

Two performers: SHOPPER and KEEPER (both male or female).

Staging: props, costumes and effects

The set needs a box or two of candles, a few cardboard boxes marked 'candles' and a counter for the shop (or a cloth-covered table). KEEPER also needs a wooden bowl, a glass of water and a single can of eels (any tin can marked 'eels') behind the counter. SHOPPER is dressed in everyday clothes; KEEPER should wear a traditional long brown shopkeeper's overcoat, if possible.

Candles in the bin

Scene: A candle shop. Boxes marked 'candles' litter the floor.
Behind the counter is a display of candles. KEEPER is
hiding (rather obviously, with legs sticking out) behind the
counter. SHOPPER spots this and approaches.

Shopper: *(Over counter)* Hello? I'm looking to buy—

Keeper: *(Holding nose)* This is a recorded
announcement... (THINKS) No one is here at
the moment. Um. Apart from you, obviously.
But if you'd like to leave a message. Well. You
can't. Sorry. (BEAT) Beep. Sorry. Ignore the
beep. The beep was for my benefit. Um.
Goodbye.

Shopper: *(Crouches down and faces KEEPER)* Hello?

Keeper: *(Leaps up; feigns confusion)* Oh, what a strange
dream. I dreamt I was an answerphone
machine. Um... that didn't take messages.

Shopper: Are you open?

Keeper: I'm frank and honest, if that's what you mean.
I'm not given to deception or concealment.
Apart from when I'm asleep. Hidden behind
the counter. Pretending to be an answerphone.

Shopper: I meant, is the shop open?

Keeper: It's closed.

Shopper: The sign on the door says 'open'.

Reproduced with permission from *All-age Sketches for the Christian Year* published by BRF 2006 (1 84101 458 3)
www.barnabasinchurches.org.uk

Keeper: It's broken. It's dangerous. Keep away.

Shopper: Do you sell candles?

Keeper: (*Laughs falsely; tries to cover up candles displayed behind him*) Dear me, no. Whatever gave you that impression?

Shopper: The shop is called 'Candles'?

Keeper: Yes. (THINKS) But that doesn't mean we sell candles. Boots doesn't sell boots, does it? You wouldn't go into Currys—the electrical shop—and order a chicken tikka masala, would you? Just because a place is called something, it doesn't mean... Selfridges! Oh, but that actually does sell fridges. Just goes to show, you never can tell...

Shopper: But this place is full of candles!

Keeper: They're decorative.

Shopper: In boxes?

Keeper: Ordered the wrong stock. I meant to order... (THINKS) Canned eels. Eels in cans. You can imagine when the delivery van pulled up. (*Acts out the scene*) 'I've got two thousand boxes of candles.' 'Candles? Don't you mean canned eels—eels in cans?' 'No, definitely candles. Cylinders or blocks of wax or tallow, with a central wick, which is lit to produce light as it burns.' 'Sorry, I wanted canned eels. Preserved snake-like fish with a slender, elongated body and poorly developed fins— proverbial for their slipperiness.' 'But the shop is called Candles!' 'Yes, but Boots is called Boots and you can't—'

Shopper: (*Impatient*) Well, seeing as you do have candles in stock. Can I buy some?

Keeper: Um. (*THINKS. Deadpan*) Yes. You. Can. (*Reaches under counter for box. Looks shifty*) Here you are.

Shopper: At last. (*Examines candles*) These candles don't appear to have any wicks…

Keeper: They're safety candles. What could be safer than a candle you can't light?

Shopper: (*Wielding a large candle as a club*) I don't know—you could use one to knock sense into a candle shopkeeper who won't sell you any candles…

Keeper: Thank goodness I'm a canned-eels shopkeeper, eh?

Shopper: (*Impatient*) Please fetch me some real candles—with wicks.

Keeper: OK. (*Reaches under counter. Produces candles*) Here you are.

Shopper: (*Examines*) Much better. Thanks. These are great.

Keeper: (*Amazed*) What on earth do you want them for?

Shopper: I'm having a romantic dinner tonight.

Keeper: Oh. Do you want any canned eels?

Shopper: No, thank you. I want candles. They create an ambience. Atmosphere. They're attractive, warm. Special. They put a scent in the air and light up a room in a way that artificial light can never replace.

Keeper: … And they come with a free bushel. *(Produces wooden bowl from under counter)*

Shopper: What's that for?

Keeper: *(Demonstrates)* You light the candle… and pop one of these on top.

Shopper: But that'll hide it. No one can appreciate the warm glow.

Keeper: Exactly.

Shopper: Isn't it dangerous putting a wooden bowl over a naked flame?

Keeper: Oh no. You see, the bushel also cuts out the oxygen and the flame snuffs out. Perfectly safe.

Shopper: You really don't get it, do you? Candles are amazing. Why do you think most people bring them out for birthdays and special occasions? Nothing can match that flickering light. That comforting flame. That glorious—

Keeper: *(Nostalgically)* I used to think like you. Used candles all the time. Loved them. Told everyone about them. Even opened a shop. *(Sighs)* But then you get a little older. It's too much of an effort. Can be quite dangerous, too. Needs a bit of attention… I don't know. I

	just sort of stopped bothering.
Shopper:	But it doesn't have to be like that…
Keeper:	Maybe it's just gone too far for me—
Shopper:	Give it a go. Rekindle that old flame. Here— let me. *(SHOPPER slowly lights the candle. KEEPER slips under the counter)* There we are. Isn't it glorious? Beautiful. *(KEEPER pops up and pours a glass of water over SHOPPER and candle. SHOPPER is drenched)* What did you do that for?
Keeper:	Sorry. Force of habit. (THINKS) As compensation—how about a free can of eels? *(Holds up can, and smiles)*

* * * END * * *

Reproduced with permission from *All-age Sketches for the Christian Year* published by BRF 2006 (1 84101 458 3)

www.barnabasinchurches.org.uk

How clean is your mind?

Curtain up

Lent starts on Ash Wednesday and comprises the 40 days (excluding the Sundays) before Easter. As the timing of Easter varies from year to year, Ash Wednesday may fall any time between the second week of February and the second week of March. However, as there is no explicit mention of Lent in it, this sketch could be used on other occasions, too, such as during a series about grace or the book of Romans.

Bible backdrop

ROMANS 6:12–14; 2 CORINTHIANS 12:9

Much like New Year resolutions, we often use Lent as an opportunity to 'clean ourselves up', bodily and spiritually. We may choose to abstain from eating chocolate, watching TV, smoking, or drinking coffee or alcohol—using the extra time to seek God and be more 'holy'. While this is a good thing, we should not mistake an act of will for the transforming power of grace. Neither must we allow self-imposed rules to become ways to get closer to God.

Sermon prompt

This sketch is loosely based on the TV show *How Clean is Your House?* presented by the bossy matriarchs Kim and Aggie. But I've tried to make it so that people with little or no knowledge of the programme can enjoy and understand the performance.

Cast

Three performers: HOLLY and JUDE, who are female or male (men in drag). These are the Kim and Aggie characters, and should be played over-the-top and pantomimesque. MONSTER (male or female). This character has no lines (just crawls on and off) but could make some monstrous noises.

Staging: props, costumes and effects

The costumes for HOLLY and JUDE can be as elaborate as you wish, but most of their clothing and cleaning props could be found around the house. HOLLY also needs a sealed envelope containing a piece of paper and JUDE needs a collection of crystals (tinfoil-covered items are a good substitute). There are lots of lines in this sketch with lengthy alliterations and tongue-twisters, which should be enunciated with relish.

How clean is your mind?

Scene: A TV show: JUDE and HOLLY enter. They are elaborately dressed as cleaning ladies, festooned with brushes, cloths, sponges and so on. HOLLY carries a mop and bucket; JUDE has a spray cleaner that she constantly uses. They both wear rubber gloves.

Jude: Good day, sin-spotters, naughtiness-noticers and filth-finders…

Holly: It's time for another edition of your favourite soul-searching makeover show…

Holly & Jude: 'How Clean is Your Mind?'

Holly: And I don't need to tell you that there are plenty of people in this very room with dirty, dirty minds.

Jude: There's some stinking synapses, filthy frontal lobes, and nasty, naughty neurons—I can see them from here! *(Sprays the air)* Pooh!

Holly: But don't fear, that means they're ripe and ready for Jude and Holly…

Jude: *(Aside)* That's us…

Holly: … to start scrubbing those synapses, cleaning out those cerebellums, and giving you a thorough brain-bath.

Jude: I'm Jude Mental.

Holly: And I'm Holly Erthanthou.

Reproduced with permission from *All-age Sketches for the Christian Year* published by BRF 2006 (1 84101 458 3)
www.barnabasinchurches.org.uk

Jude: And today we'll be showing you three tawdry tykes who've been too busy to buff up their brains…

Holly: … Too lazy to let loose on their lobes with a loo-brush…

Jude: … And too careless to clean up their cerebrums.

Holly: Jude, dear, tell us about our first smelly specimen in need of a mental makeover.

Jude: He's a 43-year-old businessman who lives in a huge, spotless house in the commuter belt. I've seen inside his mock-Tudor mansion—you'd think Brasso wouldn't melt in his mouth. Carpets fresh as the day they were laid; Y-fronts scrubbed, bleached, and neatly folded—colour-coded and labelled, laid out neatly in his undies drawer. Not a surface unwiped, not a doorknob without a covering of polish… But, dear me. A brain more neglected and left to fester you'll never see.

Holly: What are we waiting for, Jude, my dear? Let's get in there and start cleaning up this mucky mind.

Jude: You begin in his parietal lobe. I'll go on to the occipital. Good luck, Ms Erthanthou.

JUDE exits.

Holly: And you, Ms Mental. Right, well, I'm just entering his parietal lobe now and… oh, my

Reproduced with permission from *All-age Sketches for the Christian Year* published by BRF 2006 (1 84101 458 3)

www.barnabasinchurches.org.uk

giddy aunt, what's that smell? It stinks to high heaven. With my never-wrong nose— professionally trained to sniff out pongs—I'd say this was an awful build-up of avariciousness. *(Kneels and starts to examine the floor)* Oh yes, down here! You can see it! Layers and layers of sticky, stinky greed. Just take a look at that! *(Indicates grime)* Now, a lot of business types suffer from acute avarice. It's a professional hazard. But never, in all my days, have I seen it to this degree. We've got stinking-rich thoughts over here; there's a whole pile of putrid possessions, and a heap of hollow treasures he's hoarded up for himself. *(Holding nose)* Ooh, the stench.

Jude: *(Returning)* I'm back, my dear. You will not believe the utter filth I've witnessed on the other side of— *(Smell wafts over)* Oh, my unbalanced uncle! *(Sprays)* What's all this mess, Holly Erthanthou?

Holly: The biggest accumulation of cupidity I ever did see, Jude Mental.

Jude: However are we going to shift it?

Holly: A healthy dose of balance is what's needed here.

Jude: Balance?

Holly: Oh yes, dear. Balance. He needs to restore his natural flow of Chi energy by taking on a more simple existence. I suggest some meridian techniques.

Reproduced with permission from *All-age Sketches for the Christian Year* published by BRF 2006 (1 84101 458 3)
www.barnabasinchurches.org.uk

Jude: What about all his riches?

Holly: Well, he can't help that, can he? But he can clear out his cluttered mind with a sense of scale. Realize he's just a dot in an infinite universe. But it'll take a lot of hard work to keep it that way. How are you getting along, Jude, you old scrubber?

Jude: I think you got off lightly. His occipital lobe was loaded with self-importance. I can't describe the piles and piles of pongy pride paraded in front of my person. (*Sprays*) Yuck.

Holly: What did you do about it?

Jude: I applied a brand-new treatment—it's just on the market. It's called Back Down to Earth.

Holly: Oh yes, I've heard of that. It's a humility-based detergent.

Jude: Kills 99 per cent of all known conceit. Dead.

Holly: Only 99 per cent?

Jude: Nothing's 100 per cent effective, dearie.

Holly: You're too right, Jude. (*Surveys scene*) I think our work here is done, Ms Mental.

Jude: On to the next challenge, young Erthanthou.

Holly: I don't think our nasal passages will fare much better with our next victim. She's 15 years old—

Jude: Don't tell me. I know the type. Stinking teenager rotting in bed until two in the afternoon. Doesn't know one end of a roll-on deodorant from the other. Would wear the same stinky knickers every day if left to her own devices—

Holly: Oh no, dear, quite the opposite. She's one of those youngsters with a designer label fetish. Her taste is so attuned to every trend that she seldom wears the same garment twice for fear of it falling out of fashion. And the pretty princess is perpetually pampering her person with plentiful perfume—leaving her poor parents permanently... perturbed.

Jude: Right, little madam! Let's see if your neural pathways are as spotless as your personal appearance. I'll launch into the frontal lobe; you toddle over to the temporal.

Holly: Right you are, let's get scrubbing!

HOLLY exits.

Jude: Oh, my unsteady second cousin! (*Sprays*) What in the name of Daz is that? (*A slimy green MONSTER crawls into view*) A ghastly, gargantuan gorgon! A gruesome green-eyed monster if ever I saw one. An evil, backbiting little creature that has been feeding on one thing, in my experience: envy. It's going to take a lot of crystals to realign her well-being.

Holly: (*Returning*) What are you doing down there, dear? (*Spots MONSTER*) Ooh, my dopey

Reproduced with permission from *All-age Sketches for the Christian Year* published by BRF 2006 (1 84101 458 3)
www.barnabasinchurches.org.uk

daughter. Whatever's that creepy creature?

Jude: *(Producing a handful of crystals)* That, my dear, is the best-fed green-eyed monster I ever clapped my bifocals on!

Holly: And what's with all the gleaming rocks, Jude, dear?

Jude: The only cure for envy: positive vibrations. They help the young girl to love herself and be satisfied with what she's got. But she'll need to meditate hard if she wants to keep her slimy friend at bay. *(MONSTER crawls off)* How did you fare?

Holly: Not much better. Scaly monster in her frontal lobe and a hairy animal in her temporal!

Jude: What was it?

Holly: The slowest, fattest specimen of a sloth, that's what. She might permanently paint her face, and keep up with whatever colour's the new black—but she's let her PE go to pot.

Jude: Typical youngster—doesn't see the improving value of exercise. Keeps the mind focused and the body trim. *(Taps tummy)* Like mine.

Holly: That's what I thought, Ms Mental. So I've forced the female to follow a fitness formula— guaranteed to successfully see off the sloth!

Jude: Guaranteed?

Holly: Well, not quite, but if applied correctly—and with constant vigilance—it's successful in nearly

Reproduced with permission from *All-age Sketches for the Christian Year* published by BRF 2006 (1 84101 458 3)

www.barnabasinchurches.org.uk

99 per cent of cases.

Jude: Can't expect more than that. Like all our treatments, you've got to keep at it. Hard work and plenty of elbow grease—

Holly: We'll need more than that for our next victim. We'll need knee grease, arm grease, leg grease, ankle grease, wrist grease—

Jude: Calm down, love. Who is this wretched specimen?

Holly: A guest at Her Majesty's pleasure. He's in the clink. Doing porridge—

Jude: A fallen felon, eh? A common criminal. Like a piece of spat-out gum, stuck on the shoesole of society.

Holly: And with a miserable mind to match, I shouldn't wonder. But we're not the first to attempt to tidy up his excuse for a brain.

Jude: We're the clean-up queens, dear! There's no one in the business can brighten up a brain like Jude and Holly.

Holly: *(Holds up envelope)* In this envelope is the name of the new mystery treatment applied to his bonce.

Jude: I can't say I hold out much hope, Holly. Let's see. Come on. *(Sprays)* Hold your nose! *(They both enter the brain)*

Holly: *(Taken aback)* Ooh, my sure-footed stepfather, I can't believe it!

Reproduced with permission from *All-age Sketches for the Christian Year* published by BRF 2006 (1 84101 458 3)
www.barnabasinchurches.org.uk

Jude: By my unwavering auntie! We must be in the wrong brain. It's like new.

Holly: It is new, my dear. It must be. But we are in the right brain, I can assure you.

Jude: Let's take a look in that envelope, dear. And whatever this treatment is—let's hope it's not permanent, for all our sakes.

Holly: It's called GR-Ace.

Jude: GR-Ace. (THINKS) GR-Ace?

Holly: That's what it says, dear.

Jude: What's so amazing about GR-Ace? Let's have a look at that. (*Takes envelope*) Oh dear. Look what it says.

Holly & Jude: (*They gasp*) 100 per cent effective!

Holly: Quick, let's hide it away before anyone finds out.

Jude: Or there'll be no more Jude Mental.

Holly: And no Holly Erthanthou!

They run off.

* * * END * * *

Mothering Sunday

One for the ladies

Curtain up

Mothering Sunday falls on the fourth Sunday of Lent. Traditionally, this was the day when children, mainly daughters, who had gone to work as domestic servants were given a day off to visit their mother and family. As they walked along the country lanes, children would pick wild flowers or violets to take to church or give to their mother as a small gift. A cake would often be baked to celebrate the occasion, and this cake, the Simnel Cake, is now especially associated with Mothering Sunday.

Bible backdrop

GENESIS 16:1–4; 21:1–4; ROMANS 16:1–2; GALATIANS 4:21–31; 2 TIMOTHY 1:5

For many years, the fourth Sunday of Lent has been observed as Mothering Sunday in the church. The tradition arose from a passage in Galatians in which Paul uses an allegory to expound the difference between being a slave to the law (of Moses) and being free in Christ. The Jewish nation considered themselves to be descendants of Abraham, but Paul points out that true descent is spiritual, not physical. Just as Abraham's two sons were born of two mothers, one a slave (Hagar) and one a free woman (Sarah), so Abraham's true children are not those of impeccable Jewish genealogy but those whose faith is as strong as was Abraham's.

For many centuries, this passage was the Epistle reading on the fourth Sunday of Lent, and on that day people gave thanks to God for new birth and for the church, which, like a mother, nurtures God's people in the life of the Spirit.

Sermon prompt

Mothering Sunday can sometimes be a time when churches pay lip service to the female members of the congregation. It can often (not necessarily deliberately) reinforce the stereotype that women achieve fulfilment in their Christian life through marriage, childbirth and raising a family.

It can also be a painful Sunday for women who do not have children—whether through choice, medical or personal circumstances, or calling. This sketch needs to be approached with sensitivity, as it asks more questions than it answers: 'What is the unique role of women in the church? Why are women's achievements not celebrated more? Is the church's approach to women out of date?' This is not to say that we shouldn't celebrate motherhood, but rather that we should not use one Sunday of the year to try to encapsulate everything that more than half of the congregation offer to the church and the kingdom of God.

Cast

Four performers: HOST (male), an insensitive old dinosaur; JAN (female), a woman in her 30s or 40s; CAROL (female), a woman in her 20s; HELEN (female), a woman in her 40s or 50s.

Staging: props, costumes and effects

Very simple set: just four chairs, no props, and everyday clothing for all.

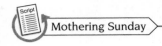
One for the ladies

Scene: HOST, a 'gentleman', is seated with three women, also seated, who are opposite him in a line: JAN, CAROL and HELEN.

Host: Hello, everyone. Welcome. Hope you are all safe and happy on this lovely Sunday. And this Sunday is especially lovely as it is a very special, special Sunday. Not for us men, of course, but for the ladies amongst us. Today—ladies and gentlemen, boys and girls—is Smothering Sunday. *(Corrects)* I mean, Mothering Sunday. A special time to focus on the lovely ladies who come along every week and serve, their work unnoticed, and their rewards forgotten. Truly, it is a thankless task, being a woman. I don't know for sure, I've never asked. But today is the day to redress the balance. This is the only day of the year when we are forced to consider all the things that the lovely ladies do for us. So, gentlemen, this is the day we don't let our attention wander and eyes glaze over when the ladies speak. Even if it is boring and irrelevant— I want all you men to grit your teeth and listen—just this once. Please. Believe me, I don't want to do this any more than you.

So, if you're wondering who these three strangers are on stage with me—I'll tell you.

They are ladies. But, more surprisingly, they are ladies with something to say. I have asked these three fine fillies to join me and speak a little about themselves. First, lovely Jan. Hello, lovely Jan.

Jan: Hello.

Host: Now, lovely Jan, what would you like to spend your two to two and a half minutes talking to us about today?

Jan: I'd like to talk about God's heart for the poor.

Host: Isn't that lovely? Jan would like to talk about God's heart for poor women.

Jan: Just God's heart for the poor.

Host: Great. God's heart for the poor, from a woman's perspective.

Jan: From my perspective.

Host: From Jan's perspective, as a woman—

Jan: *(Irritated)* Sorry. God's heart for the poor. That's what I'm talking about. And that's it.

Host: That told me, eh, lads? Best not to argue with them, not when they're like that. Next up is Carol. Now, I know what you want to fill your two to two and a half minutes up with—you want to talk about your calling with children.

Carol: Yes.

Host: Now, tell me, Carol, how many little darlings do you have?

Reproduced with permission from *All-age Sketches for the Christian Year* published by BRF 2006 (1 84101 458 3)

www.barnabasinchurches.org.uk

Carol: No, I think you've misunderstood. I don't have any children—

Host: Oh, I see—you're feeling a bit clucky? Carol? Broody? Want to get a few nippers under your belt? Clock's ticking, isn't it, Carol? What does the old man indoors think?

Carol: I'm not married.

Host: I can see a bit of a problem here, Carol. You need to find yourself a fine gentleman if you want to start breeding—

Carol: No. I want to work with other children. Not my own. Street children in Brazil.

Host: Get some practice in, eh? Maybe find yourself a fella while you're out there?

Carol: No, I'm doing it because that's where God has called me. That's what he's laid on my heart for me to do. I'm not sure I'll ever get married, or have children of my own—

Host: Oh. Right. But this is Smother… I mean, Mothering Sunday. I'm not sure where you fit in. At least we still have Helen who, as I can tell by the sparkler and rings on her left hand, has already taken the nuptial plunge. You're here to talk about marriage, is that right?

Helen: In a manner of speaking. My husband walked out on me three years ago. I'd like to talk about how isolating it can be when you are single and all your friends seem to be happily married.

Host: While I'm sure that would be a wonderful thing to talk about, Helen, I don't think this is really the time or place. This is a happy day for the rest of us. We are here to celebrate the glorious, wonderful things that being a lady in church can offer. Can't it wait? You've obviously carried this secret guilt for a long time. What's another few weeks, eh?

Helen: I think it's just as valid talking about how difficult it is—

Host: Thanks, Helen. Just not this particular day. It's a day for us to learn about the valuable role God has for women, as mothers.

Carol: Why not talk about the valuable contribution of women?

Host: Because we can do that any Sunday.

Jan: But we don't.

Host: The fact that we don't has no bearing on this Sunday, Smother— I mean, Mothering Sunday. This is the week that we talk about women who are mothers.

Helen: So, what do you want us to talk about?

Host: I was hoping that one of you could tell us about the valuable contribution of women as mothers.

Jan: Why us?

Host: Because you are women!

Carol: Why don't you just talk, if you think it's that important?

Reproduced with permission from *All-age Sketches for the Christian Year* published by BRF 2006 (1 84101 458 3)

www.barnabasinchurches.org.uk

Host: Of course, I could. I'm happy to talk about the role of men any time. Just not this Sunday. This is Ladies' Sunday.

Helen: I think what Carol was saying was, why don't you talk about the valuable role of women?

Host: What like?

Jan: Think.

Host: Um. Cleaning?

Carol: Men can do that, too.

Host: Bringing up children?

Helen: Men do that, too.

Host: Flower arranging?

Jan: And that.

Host: Umm. Umm. Shoes?

Carol: What about them?

Host: Shoe selection? Shoe accumulation? Shoe—

Helen: Valuable things? Valuable contributions that women can bring? What has God given to women? What is distinctive? Different? Unique?

Host: I... I... I... I... don't know!

Jan: Maybe it's time you found out.

Host: How?

Helen: Listening...

Jan: Talking...

Carol: Empathizing...

Reproduced with permission from *All-age Sketches for the Christian Year* published by BRF 2006 (1 84101 458 3)
www.barnabasinchurches.org.uk

Host: All at once?

Helen: Multi-tasking...

Host: On my own?

Jan: Sharing...

Host: What if I'm not up to it?

Carol: Being vulnerable...

Host: I don't know what to say.

Helen: Try talking about your feelings...

Host: Feelings? (PAUSE) I'm sorry, but (*Looks at watch*) thank heavens, that's the ten-minute 'ladies' slot' over for another year. So we can forget about all this nonsense for another twelve months. Back to the proper programme next week. (*To the women*) I'd better let you all go, hadn't I? Don't want to make you late putting the Sunday dinner on...

* * * END * * *

Dangerous donkey

Curtain up

Palm Sunday falls on the first day of Holy Week, the Sunday before
Easter Day.

Bible backdrop

MATTHEW 21:1–11

Jesus' triumphal entry into Jerusalem on a donkey marks the
beginning of the week leading up to his trial and death. The village
of Bethphage is mentioned only in connection with this story. The
donkey is symbolic of humility, peace and Davidic royalty (see
Zechariah 9:9). Matthew mentions two animals, while the other
Gospels only mention one.

Sermon prompt

Using Matthew's account, this sketch takes a sideways look at the
events of Palm Sunday, from the point of view of the two donkeys that
Jesus used to make his triumphal entry into Jerusalem. Of course, we
don't know anything about the background of these donkeys, but
this perspective offers a fresh approach to the celebration.

In the sketch, the mother (DONKEY) considers her son (COLT)
to be insignificant. But we know from the biblical stories of Moses,
David, Gideon, Peter and so on that it is often the most unlikely or
overlooked people that God chooses to carry out his plans. The
story is also about being obedient to our calling. Sometimes God
will ask us to do something that may seem strange or insignificant,

and only when we have been obedient will God reveal his bigger plan.

In addition, the sketch examines how Jesus rose from his humble birth (when he was also carried on a donkey) to the events of Palm Sunday when he was welcomed into Jerusalem as the new king. It is an opportunity to ask people what God is calling them to—particularly if it is something new or unusual—and to urge them, if it is from God, to take up the challenge so that God can reveal even greater plans.

Cast

Two performers: DONKEY and COLT (female and male).

Staging: props, costumes and effects

Either have lots of fun creating elaborate costumes for the two characters or use a few signifiers such as big donkey's ears and long noses. Very little is needed for a set, and the only prop is the sealed letter that COLT is clutching, containing his secret mission from 'Dangerous Donkeys', which is opened by DONKEY.

Dangerous donkey

Scene: A village outside Jerusalem around AD33. DONKEY (a donkey) waits impatiently for her son, COLT (a young donkey), to return. She is not happy.

Colt: *(Excited)* Mum, Mum! I'm back!

Donkey: *(Cross)* Nice of you to drop by. Where do you think I've been all morning?

Colt: *(Ignoring)* I've been given my first assignment!

Donkey: I'll tell you where I've been: stuck down a well!

Colt: Just imagine! My very first mission from Dangerous Donkeys: 'For donkeys that dare to do what other donkeys don't'!

Donkey: Are you listening to me? While you were out 'embarking on your new employment', your poor mother was stuck in a disgusting ditch. Someone must have dug a pit and forgot to cover it up—there ought to be a law against it!

Colt: Oh, the well! I saw it when I went past on my way to the Dangerous Donkeys secret HQ. I'm sure it was covered with palm branches...

Donkey: When I fell in, it wasn't covered with palm branches!

Colt: You know, that reminds me. There was a big crowd of people carrying palms, waving them

Reproduced with permission from *All-age Sketches for the Christian Year* published by BRF 2006 (1 84101 458 3)
www.barnabasinchurches.org.uk

about and shouting. Maybe they picked up the branches covering the well. Seemed to be quite a celebration. I think they were marching to Jerusalem.

Donkey: That's where you should be heading, you layabout! Jerusalem! Where the action is. Where important people go. Not skulking about here, wasting your life. Mind you, if you *had been* here, you could at least have helped me out of the well…

Colt: Why didn't the master help you out?

Donkey: It's the sabbath, you dumb ass! He would have left me there until Monday if I hadn't managed to scramble up the side.

Colt: But you are OK now, aren't you? Anyway, I have some fantastic news!

Donkey: He never liked me, that master. I'm sure he's coveting that donkey next door.

Colt: You know how you're always saying how useless I am, and I'll never amount to anything—

Donkey: Some master! He won't even untie me from the stall and lead me to water on the sabbath.

Colt: I had an interview this very morning—and they offered me a job.

Donkey: When I finally shuffle off this mortal coil, I suspect the master will just drag me away and throw me outside the gates of Jerusalem!

Reproduced with permission from *All-age Sketches for the Christian Year* published by BRF 2006 (1 84101 458 3)

www.barnabasinchurches.org.uk

Colt: (*Continuing*) I'm now an official Dangerous Donkey agent. And today I was given my first assignment!

Donkey: You? A Dangerous Donkey? Huh! I don't believe it.

Colt: Here it is in black and white. (*Shows envelope*)

Donkey: Now, my father, on the other hand—your grandfather—he was a brave, bold donkey. Legend has it he carried our Lord, still in his mother's womb, across hundreds of miles to Bethlehem. He was there when the angels came, then the shepherds, and the wise men. They even wrote a song about him! (*Starts singing 'Little donkey'*)

Colt: Don't you even want to know what it is?

Donkey: And when Mary and Joseph had to take the baby Jesus into exile—under threat of death—who carried them to Egypt? Your grandfather, that's who!

Colt: I'm very proud of Grandpa, you know that. But aren't you even curious about my assignment?

Donkey: What is it?

Colt: I don't know. I haven't read it yet.

Donkey: Give it here, you mule! (*Takes paper. Opens and reads. Replies sarcastically*) Dangerous Donkeys, eh?

Colt: 'For donkeys that dare to do what…'

Donkey: '… other donkeys don't.' I know.

Reproduced with permission from *All-age Sketches for the Christian Year* published by BRF 2006 (1 84101 458 3)
www.barnabasinchurches.org.uk

Colt: What is it? Do I have to go undercover at the court of King Herod? Or lead a rebellion against the Roman oppressors? Or bite a Samaritan on the bottom?

Donkey: *(Reading)* 'Here is your top-secret special assignment Dangerous Donkey agent codename: The Ass-assin—'

Colt: I chose the nickname. Do you like it?

Donkey: Let me finish: 'You are to head to Bethphage on the Mount of Olives…'

Colt: Up high, yes. A strategic position to view the surrounding countryside. I suspect it's an ambush of some sort—probably a raid on Jerusalem.

Donkey: 'Then go on to the village ahead of you…'

Colt: The village. Of course. Inconspicuous. What could be more innocent-looking than a wandering donkey in a sleepy village?

Donkey: 'Once you have entered the village you will find a post…'

Colt: A post. Good disguise. I suspect it's the next checkpoint.

Donkey: 'There, at the post, you will tie yourself up…'

Colt: And receive further orders, right?

Donkey: Nope.

Colt: Oh, I'll soon be joined by a whole squad of Dangerous Donkeys, right?

www.barnabasinchurches.org.uk

Donkey: Wrong.

Colt: What else does it say?

Donkey: Nothing.

Colt: Nothing at all?

Donkey: That's it.

Colt: Oh, that's a little... disappointing.

Donkey: Disappointing? It's downright dull! Your top-secret assignment: Go to some tiny hamlet, tie yourself up and hang about? It's hardly what I'd call dangerous!

Colt: It's a start. It could be a test. If I do this, maybe I'll get given a bigger challenge.

Donkey: What, like having a brisk walk down a dusty track? Or wearing a straw hat by the seaside?

Colt: Let me read it. *(Takes paper)*

Donkey: And to think your grandfather carried the Messiah, the Son of Man, the Anointed One... What is this family coming to? I've a good mind to show you the back of my hoof.

Colt: There's a PS at the bottom. *(Reads)* There is something else I have to do.

Donkey: Is it dangerous?

Colt: Well, I think it is. It says, '... and don't forget to bring along your mum'.

Donkey: What do they want me for? I ask you! We ought to be off collecting palm leaves like everybody else today. There's something

Reproduced with permission from *All-age Sketches for the Christian Year* published by BRF 2006 (1 84101 458 3)
www.barnabasinchurches.org.uk

82

exciting going on—and they're heading to Jerusalem. I've heard there's a very important person coming. The most important person— our new king. He's coming to Jerusalem to set us all free. And where are we headed?

Colt: Somewhere else?

Donkey: Exactly. Useless.

Colt: But you know who they say is coming?

Donkey: Who?

Colt: Jesus. Just think, that same fragile little baby— born in a stable—is coming here as a triumphant king! From the humblest beginnings to glory! So it just goes to show... you've got to start somewhere. And that's what I'm doing.

Donkey: Let's just get on with it. We might catch the end of the celebrations once your 'exciting' mission is completed. You're a fool of a donkey!

Colt: No. I'm a foal of a donkey.

Donkey: I know what I said. We're going to miss everything!

* * * END * * *

Reproduced with permission from *All-age Sketches for the Christian Year* published by BRF 2006 (1 84101 458 3)
www.barnabasinchurches.org.uk

Fair's fair

Curtain up

Good Friday is the Friday before Easter, and is the day when Christians commemorate the suffering and death of Jesus. It is the most solemn day in the Christian year and most churches mark the day with a time of quiet and reflection. This sketch could be used as part of a Good Friday reflection, or on any occasion to remind people of their first encounter with Jesus.

Bible backdrop

MATTHEW 5:8; 27:31–54

The cross is central to the Christian faith, and all Christians have at one time—metaphorically and spiritually—met Jesus at the foot of the cross. It is in response to his sacrifice that the cross is the cornerstone of our faith, and we are encouraged to return to the symbol of the cross to keep our concerns in perspective. However, it is all too easy to forget that initial encounter with Jesus. Our lives tend to drift into revolving around our concerns, our preferences, our expectations of church and our lives.

Sermon prompt

This is a fairly serious sketch to suit the subject matter: Jesus' crucifixion. The sketch asks about the kinds of concerns that 'experienced' Christians bring to Jesus—our petty squabbles, unforgiveness and lifestyle wants—and contrasts them with the experience of a new Christian, discovering grace, forgiveness and acceptance for the first time.

Cast

Four performers: ONE and TWO (male or female), 'experienced' Christians coming to Jesus with their prayer requests; THREE (male or female), someone coming to meet Jesus at the cross for the first time; JESUS (male) has no dialogue and needs to be played sensitively.

Staging: props, costumes and effects

ONE carries an umbrella. ONE and TWO should be in their 'Sunday best', while THREE is in casual clothes. I suggest that JESUS wears black (black trousers and top).

Fair's fair

Scene: A desert. ONE stands as if starting a queue. TWO approaches.

One: Good afternoon.

Two: Nice day for it.

One: Speak for yourself. *(Puts up umbrella)* It's scorching out here. I'm glad I brought my sun umbrella.

Two: Don't want to be out in this heat for too long, that's for sure.

One: Absolutely. (BEAT) Now, we need to get a few things straight.

Two: Don't fret. I'm not going to take your place. You were here first. I know that.

One: I don't mean to be officious.

Two: *(Aside)* It just comes naturally.

One: So long as we're all agreed.

PAUSE.

Two: Two minutes enough for you?

One: Two minutes—?

Two: There are people behind you, you know. I don't want to be here all afternoon.

Reproduced with permission from *All-age Sketches for the Christian Year* published by BRF 2006 (1 84101 458 3)
www.barnabasinchurches.org.uk

One: I have a number of things to say, that's all—

Two: Two minutes should be enough—

One: These things take time—

Two: That's all you gave me last time. Two minutes. Of course, that was when I was at front of the queue…

One: Oh, very well.

Three: *(Running up, out of breath)* Is he here yet?

One: *(Dismissive)* Patience is a virtue, you know. He will come. All in good time.

Three: *(Breathes out)* Thank goodness. *(Falls to his knees)*

Two: There is a queue.

Three: *(To himself)* If I can just touch—

Two: *(Getting THREE's attention)* I say. This is a queue. We are in a queue.

One: *(To TWO)* First timer. Oh dear.

Two: Don't you know?

Three: Oh—I've got so much to say—

One: You can't kneel there, you know.

Two: This is the queue. *(Points)* One. Two. I'm two. If you want to be three, get in line.

Three: I didn't think there would be a queue—

One: Well, there is.

Two: And we were here first.

One: *(Clears throat)* I am first.

Reproduced with permission from *All-age Sketches for the Christian Year* published by BRF 2006 (1 84101 458 3)

www.barnabasinchurches.org.uk

Two: And I am second.

Three: I didn't think that he—

One: It's not his idea.

Two: It's ours.

Three: But surely he—?

One: We don't need to bother him with it. The important thing is, there is a queue. Fair's fair.

Three: OK. I don't mind waiting. I just have so much to say—

Two: Two minutes.

Three: Sorry?

One: That's all you get.

Three: I'm not sure I can explain it all in two minutes—

Two: Well, you'll have to.

One: Fair's fair.

Three: But I'm not sure I can—

Two: Do you mind? Try to consider other people for a change, can't you?

One: *(To TWO)* First timers! *(Tuts)*

Three: Sorry. I'm not used to all this. I just thought that he would accept anyone. That's what I've been told—

One: Oh. He would. Too kind for his own good sometimes.

Two: That's why we've set up a few rules.

Reproduced with permission from *All-age Sketches for the Christian Year* published by BRF 2006 (1 84101 458 3)
www.barnabasinchurches.org.uk

One: Bit of order. So we all know where we are.

Two: He's not an organizer.

One: Not his thing. Bit of a loose cannon, if you ask me.

Two: Did you hear about his antics in the temple?

One: Went on the rampage, from what I'm told. So it's up to us to provide a bit of order.

Two: We set up this queue, so we all know where we are.

One: And we each get two minutes. Fair's fair. First it's me.

Two: Then it's me.

One: Then you.

Three: I'm not sure I'll be able to manage it in just two minutes—I'm so excited!

Two: *(Deadpan, to ONE)* He's excited.

One: *(To TWO, shakes head)* First timers. They always are.

Two: *(To ONE)* He'll get over it.

One: *(To THREE)* I'm sure you are very excited. But we've been here a long, long time. (BEAT) Longer than you.

Two: And we know what's what.

One: So be good and wait your turn.

Two: Then we'll all know where we are. And what's what.

Reproduced with permission from *All-age Sketches for the Christian Year* published by BRF 2006 (1 84101 458 3)

www.barnabasinchurches.org.uk

One: (BEAT) Fair's fair…

Three: *(In wonder)* Here he comes—

JESUS comes over quietly and stands a short distance away. He stretches out his arms like a cross.

One: Here we go. Now remember what we said. *(To THREE)* Get in the queue. My turn first.

Two: Two minutes, remember.

One: I know. *(Steps up to the cross; puts on even posher voice)* Oh, your mighty, majestic magnificence…

Three: *(Bursting out)* I can't believe I'm here! And he's here!

One: Do you mind? *(Scratches head)* Oh. Now. Where was I?

Two: *(Looking at watch)* One minute and thirty seconds left…

One: But he interrupted!

Two: That's not my fault.

Three: I'm really sorry—

One: Just keep quiet, can't you?

Two: One minute fifteen seconds.

One: Oh, for goodness'— Right. Where was I? Oh, your mightiness etcetera. Now. Sunday last. I'm sure you noticed, but when the vicar came up to speak he blew his nose on a handkerchief. *(Incredulous)* A handkerchief! In front of the whole church. Now

Reproduced with permission from *All-age Sketches for the Christian Year* published by BRF 2006 (1 84101 458 3)
www.barnabasinchurches.org.uk

I'm not saying he's… you know… (*Looks over shoulder; whispers*) in sin. But what does that say about a man's character? He should have blown it discreetly in the gentlemen's rest room before the commencement of the service. Or waited until afterwards. I don't want to be subjected to bodily functions during a sermon on Leviticus—

Two: (*Steps forward*) Time's up.

One: Excuse me. I haven't finished. I was distracted.

Two: (*Snide*) Fair's fair.

One: But I was interrupted—

Two: What's the point of having rules if—?

One: I want an extra 30 seconds.

Two: We won't know where we are if—

Three: Oh, I can't wait any longer. (*Steps forward*) I'm so, so sorry. Please forgive me—

Two: Now he's started!

One: Just let me finish!

Three: If you can find it in your heart to somehow—

Two: (*Pushing in front of THREE*) Greetings, your most wonderfulness. Now. I need to talk to you about my conservatory. The thing is, I really want it to be done by next Thursday. The builder seems to be taking an age. Can't you speed things up a bit?

One: (*Jostling with TWO*) Don't listen! It's my turn and I haven't finished! It's not the fact that he sneezed—

Reproduced with permission from *All-age Sketches for the Christian Year* published by BRF 2006 (1 84101 458 3)

www.barnabasinchurches.org.uk

Three: My lord! My king! My saviour! Have pity on me! Save me!

Two: We've got people over on Friday. And it would be a weight off my mind—

One: I mentioned it to him afterwards and he didn't seem to listen. It's the principle. I mean, who wants to witness that sort of spectacle on a Sunday?

Two: And the price seems to be going up and up. I'm prepared to pay my way. But you expect things to be done on schedule—

One: Some great red conk being emptied into a dirty old snot-rag. It's not decent!

Two: Wednesday would be better. But Thursday at the latest—I'd like to put the ornaments out. Make it look nice, you know?

Three: Please, please… please… *(Starts to sob)* Forgive me!

JESUS comes down from the cross, embraces THREE and raises him to his feet.

One: It's the children I worry about. And the older people. And decent people. Polite people. *(Pushes TWO away)* Like myself.

Two: Do you mind!

One: I beg your pardon!

Two: You've had your go. You're hogging it!

Reproduced with permission from *All-age Sketches for the Christian Year* published by BRF 2006 (1 84101 458 3)
www.barnabasinchurches.org.uk

One: If anyone's a hog, it's you! Piggy!

Two: That's rich coming from a stuck-up, rat-faced old toffee-nose like you!

JESUS leads THREE away, leaving ONE and TWO arguing.

One: Piggy!

Two: Rat face!

One: Piggy!

Two: Rat face!

One: (*Looks up*) He's gone!

Two: Of all the cheek!

One: See you back here next time?

Two: Not if I see you first. (*Storms off*)

* * * END * * *

Reproduced with permission from *All-age Sketches for the Christian Year* published by BRF 2006 (1 84101 458 3)

www.barnabasinchurches.org.uk

Won't you roll away the stone?

Curtain up

Easter celebrates the resurrection of Jesus Christ. It is the most important Christian festival, and the one celebrated with the greatest joy. The date of Easter changes each year. The calculation dates back to the Council of Nicea in AD325, when it was decided that Easter should fall on the Sunday following the first vernal new moon, thus linking Easter to the Jewish Passover festival.

As the sketch is about Lazarus, it could also be used when studying John 11:1–44.

Bible backdrop

MARK 16:1–8

Resurrection is a funny thing. If it happened to our next-door neighbour, we'd be shocked, incredulous, dumbfounded. Yet, somehow, Christ's resurrection has been diminished by its familiarity: in a way, we *expect* Jesus to rise from the dead—that's what he's supposed to do.

Sermon prompt

To make real the astonishing event of Jesus' victory over death, this sketch parallels the event with the story of Lazarus, an ordinary man to whom an extraordinary thing happened. Through this, we can experience some of the amazement of the people who first heard about Jesus' resurrection.

The sketch also discusses some of the theories that people have put forward to explain Jesus' return to life: he was asleep or in a coma, the disciples or the Romans stole the body, and so on (all of which are rapidly dismissed).

Cast

Three performers: OWNER (male or female), who adopts a series of pseudonyms depending on which of his dodgy businesses he is fronting; DEPUTY (male or female) disappears for the bulk of the sketch, but returns at the end; LAZARUS (male), a man surprised to be in the land of the living.

Staging: props, costumes and effects

All the characters should be dressed in mock-Roman or 'ancient biblical world' garb—robes, sandals and so on. The set is a simple reception desk, sporting a highly anachronistic telephone, for which I make no excuse (it serves its narrative purpose). You may have to explain to the children that there were no advanced tele-communication devices in AD33, but also tell them about the aqueduct to balance things out.

Won't you roll away the stone?

Scene: Reception of Flavius' Funeral Service. OWNER is behind the reception desk, upon which there is a telephone. OWNER is giving instructions to DEPUTY.

Owner: This is a very important contract. Vital. Pivotal. Are you listening? *(Silence)* Well?

Deputy: Of course I'm—

Owner: You're not listening! You're talking!

Deputy: I am listening—

Owner: You are talking now! Right? Are you listening?

Deputy: *(Tentative)* Yes—

LAZARUS enters.

Owner: There you go again, talking! Now get going. I've got a customer. And I don't want to hear that something has gone wrong. Are you listening?

Deputy: Of course—

Owner: There you go again, talking! Get going. *(Turns to LAZARUS)* How can I help you, sir?

Lazarus: Hello. I'm looking for a Mr Flavius.

Owner: Yes, that's right. Flavius' Funeral Services: 'You pop your clogs, we fit your togs.'

Lazarus: Togs?

Reproduced with permission from *All-age Sketches for the Christian Year* published by BRF 2006 (1 84101 458 3)
www.barnabasinchurches.org.uk

Owner: Burial shroud. Not very clear, is it? We're still working on a motto.

Lazarus: I see. Now, it's about a funeral—

Owner: Has one of your friends passed on?

Lazarus: Not exactly. That is to say, someone died but—

Owner: No, no, no, sir. We do not use such words here. Our absent friends are resting; they have joined the angels. They are immortally challenged.

Lazarus: Whatever. The thing is… it's a bit complicated. (*Phone rings*)

Owner: Sorry, can I get that? (*LAZARUS nods*) Hello, which service would you like? Taxidermy? Tacitus' Taxidermy: 'You snuff it, we stuff it.' A camel? How many humps? Sorry. Can't do anything that size until next week. Unless you want him to have one floppy hump? No? Thank you. Goodbye. (*To LAZARUS*) It's a nightmare. Just taken on too many contracts for the Roman authorities. You were funerals, weren't you? 'You pop your clogs—'

Lazarus: You fit the togs, yes. The thing is, I'd like to request a refund—

Owner: Refund? If it was not up to your satisfaction—

Lazarus: No. It just didn't turn out to be, um, necessary after all…

Owner: After all?

Lazarus: And I'd like a refund. At least a part refund. I'll

Reproduced with permission from *All-age Sketches for the Christian Year* published by BRF 2006 (1 84101 458 3)

www.barnabasinchurches.org.uk

pay the embalming costs. But we don't need the tomb any more.

Owner: Now. Listen here. We don't do refunds for funerals. And we don't give money back on tombs.

Lazarus: Why not?

Owner: Because in this line of business, when you fit a dearly departed with a resting place, they tend to stay there. We haven't had a single dissatisfied customer. That is to say, no one has ever come back to complain. *(Phone rings)* Sorry about this.

Which service, please? Claudius' Crematorium: 'You kill it, we grill it.' How can I help? Yes, that will be fine for next Wednesday. Would you like a psalm to be read when your future fried friend departs? Psalm 119? That one does cost a little extra. Ten pieces of silver. You'd prefer a budget option? How much were you intending to spend? One piece of silver? Ah. Can I recommend Psalm 117? Oh yes, it's much the same sentiment as 119. Just a little more… (THINKS) Pithy. Great. See you on Wednesday. Remember to bring the dearly departed. I know. But I always say it because you'd be surprised how many people forget. Bye. *(To LAZARUS)* Now, where were we?

Lazarus: My refund?

Owner: We don't do refunds. People who call upon our

Reproduced with permission from *All-age Sketches for the Christian Year* published by BRF 2006 (1 84101 458 3)
www.barnabasinchurches.org.uk

98

funerary expertise always take up the service.

Lazarus: Yes, but this is different—

Owner: OK. I'll check the records. What is the name of the deceased?

Lazarus: Lazarus.

Owner: Laelia, Laurentia, Laurentius… here it is, Lazarus. Buried two weeks ago. And your name is?

Lazarus: Lazarus.

Owner: Oh. Are you related?

Lazarus: In a manner of speaking—

Owner: (*Sighs*) What is your relation to the deceased?

Lazarus: I am the deceased. (*Phone rings*)

Owner: You're mad! Even if you are, a deal is a deal. You paid for the tomb; you lie in it—if you get my meaning.

Lazarus: It's nothing like that—

Owner: Not Joseph of Arimathea, is it? He's already tried to steal our trade. Offering his tomb to all and sundry. Stole another client off us last week, old Joseph. But it wasn't a dead loss, if you'll pardon the expression. We won the security contract…

Lazarus: Security contract?

Owner: Guarding the tomb.

Lazarus: Who from?

Owner: This particular late lamented was a bit of a fanatical fundamentalist. Lots of followers of his might want to steal the body, apparently—

Lazarus: Steal the body?

Owner: Yeah, and put a rumour about that he's planning to come back from the dead. You'd know all about that. Tax dodge, was it? There's a lot of nutters about, you know. But I'm not worried about guarding this tomb. Last I heard, his followers had all run away in fright. Even his right-hand man had scarpered.

Lazarus: And you're there to stop them getting in—?

Owner: That's what they are paying us for. Oh, and the corpse getting out—

Lazarus: Getting out?

Owner: I know. It's madness. But they're paying five silver pieces a day, so I'm not arguing.

Lazarus: Are they sure he's dead? Maybe he's sleeping...

Owner: Only euphemistically. No, this one's popped it. Public execution. First he was beaten, flogged, paraded through the streets, then nailed to a bit of two by four and left to die in public. Even then they weren't satisfied. Ran him through with a spear just to make sure—which makes you wonder why they want so much security. It's not like he's coming back. As a matter of fact, I've just sent one of my staff to check on it. (BEAT) But we still haven't sorted out your little complaint.

Reproduced with permission from *All-age Sketches for the Christian Year* published by BRF 2006 (1 84101 458 3)
www.barnabasinchurches.org.uk

Lazarus: It's a bit difficult to explain…

Owner: Try me.

Lazarus: The thing is, a few weeks ago I fell ill and, um, died—

Owner: What did you say?

Lazarus: Sorry, I'd passed over to the other side…

Deputy: *(Bursts in)* Sorry. Boss? Can I have a word?

Owner: I can hear talking again. I'm rather interested in what this nutcase has got to say for himself—

Deputy: But it's important!

Owner: You're not listening…

Deputy: I am listening!

Owner: Talking!

Deputy: (BEAT) It's about money.

Owner: Excuse me one moment, Mr Lazarus. *(To DEPUTY)* Right, *I'm* listening…

Deputy: You know this tomb you sent me to check? The one where we're doing the security…

Owner: Routine stuff. Open-and-shut case—

Deputy: I'm afraid it's open again—

Owner: You what? What about that massive boulder I told you to roll over the entrance?

Deputy: It's shifted.

Owner: By whom, the Romans?

Deputy: Why would they do that? They're the ones who wanted it guarded—

Owner: Oh, I know that. I'm clutching at straws. You know what this means? They won't pay us. And you know how I hate losing money. What about the body?

Deputy: Gone.

Owner: What?

Deputy: The tomb was empty.

Owner: Must have been nicked.

Deputy: No. There's a strange rumour going around. People are saying he's come back from the dead.

Owner: But that's impossible! I'll give you five pieces of silver if you can name me one other person who's come back from the dead—

Lazarus: Perhaps I could help you with that one...

Owner: Ah, Mr Lazarus. You have a habit of popping up unexpectedly. You say you were dead?

Lazarus: Yes, but—

Owner: Then you came back. (*Sighs*) How are you feeling?

Lazarus: Oh, fine. Now.

Owner: But you will rejoin the ranks of the choir invisible some time?

Lazarus: Oh yes. I'm not immortal.

Reproduced with permission from *All-age Sketches for the Christian Year* published by BRF 2006 (1 84101 458 3)
www.barnabasinchurches.org.uk

Owner: Good. Excellent news. That means you will be requiring my services at some point in the future?

Lazarus: Absolutely. I mean, I can't fault your workmanship. Those bandages were very well wrapped. Took an age to wriggle out. Most embarrassing, what with all those people watching—

Owner: So, shall we call it a trial run? I'll keep the tomb ready for when you decide to permanently shuffle off this mortal coil. And there will be no charge for the next ceremony. Call it two for the price of one.

Lazarus: To tell you the truth, I'd rather have the refund.

Owner: And that would be over my dead body!

Lazarus: (*Leaving*) Whatever you say!

* * * END * * *

Christian Aid Week

In for a penny...

Curtain up

Christian Aid Week usually falls in the second week of May. It is the largest house-to-house collection in the UK, with the involvement of over 300,000 volunteers and 20,000 local churches. Many schools mark the week with extra-curricular fund-raising events. Since its foundation in 1945, Christian Aid has given money and support to hundreds of life-changing projects in more than 60 countries. Today, Christian Aid helps those who live in the UK and Ireland to understand and tackle the root causes of poverty. It gives people a way to be involved in making the world a fairer place.

Although this sketch is primarily for Christian Aid Week, it could be used any time a church or group wishes to highlight God's heart for the poor (such as Maundy Thursday) and the injustice of how people in poverty are treated across the world. It is a sketch to start discussions and highlight issues as much as to suggest a solution.

Bible backdrop

LEVITICUS 25:8–12; ISAIAH 61:1–2; LUKE 4:16–21

The Israelites counted their years in groups of seven. Every seventh year was designated a sabbatical year, when agricultural land was rested from farming. After seven times seven years, there was an additional sabbath year called the Jubilee, or year of forgiveness (atonement). In that year, all the land that had changed ownership during the previous 49 years was returned to its original owner. In this way, a just and fair distribution of land was preserved, in which the poor were prevented from losing their property for ever and the rich were prevented from gaining control of the country through the accumulation of land. This principle was the inspiration for Jubilee 2000, the campaign that persuaded governments and banks to release the poorest countries of the world from their crippling debts.

The principle of Jubilee is threaded through the book of Isaiah and proclaimed by Jesus in his special care for those who are cast out by society. Yet still today the poorest countries in the world are forced to pay over $100 million each day to the rich world in debt repayments. Meanwhile, poverty kills millions of their people and creditors force poor countries to privatize their services, open up their markets or cut essential spending.

Stage prompt

This sketch sets out to personalize and reveal on an individual level what debt repayments do to vulnerable people and their countries. But this is not a sombre piece—it aims to raise the issues in a light-hearted way to reveal the absurdity of the situation. And it has a happy ending.

Cast

Three performers: HOMELESS and BUSINESS (both male or female) and PASSER (male or female), who represents God and God working through us as individuals to demand fairer treatment of the poor.

Staging: props, costumes and effects

HOMELESS, clearly, should be dressed in a humble way, but please refrain from making the character a caricature 'tramp'. BUSINESS, on the other hand, should be signified as much as possible by the stereotype of a city commuter or business person: sharp suit, umbrella, briefcase or laptop bag. In contrast, PASSER is an everyday figure, so should be dressed in casual clothes. There are a few small props such as a newspaper, a plastic cup and some loose change, but nothing that can't be found around the house.

In for a penny...

Scene: HOMELESS is sitting cross-legged, with a sleeping bag wrapped around, holding a plastic cup. In front is a makeshift sign: 'HUNGRY'. PASSER walks by and drops a pound coin into the cup.

Homeless: Cheers, mate. God bless you.

BUSINESS approaches, with a copy of the Financial Times under arm. Examines HOMELESS.

Homeless: *(Slightly wary)* All right, there?

Business: *(Cheery)* Oh yes, very well. How are you getting along?

Homeless: *(Looks in cup)* Not bad, you know.

Business: You don't remember me?

Homeless: I'm afraid lots of people come past here on the way to the station. That's why I picked this spot—

Business: I was here last week. I distinctly remember: you were sat here as you are now, opposite the Jubilee line. I was about to catch a train. Walking along... *(Demonstrates; HOMELESS looks blank)* Possibly whistling? *(Whistles)* And then... Kerr-ching! I popped a pound in the pot. *(Enthusiastically mimes putting a coin in the cup)*

Reproduced with permission from *All-age Sketches for the Christian Year* published by BRF 2006 (1 84101 458 3)
www.barnabasinchurches.org.uk

Homeless: Oh, you gave us a pound last week? Oh, thanks—

Business: *(Looks proud)* There's no need to thank me.

Homeless: Well, thanks—

Business: No need!

Homeless: No, but anyway, thanks—

Business: *(Waves finger, shakes head)* Uh-uh. No need.

Homeless: OK.

PAUSE

Business: *(Looks disappointed)* That is to say, a little gratitude wouldn't go amiss…

Homeless: Sorry. It's really appreciated. I don't know what I'd do without people like you. I know you don't have to do it. Everyone's hurrying for a train. It's easy to walk past. So… thanks.

Business: So, what did you do with it? The pound?

Homeless: I don't know. I—

Business: *(Indignant)* You don't know? One second it's all gratitude and the next—

Homeless: Last week, you say? Let me think…

Business: Thursday. 'Bout six o'clock?

Homeless: *(Feigning remembrance)* Oh, yeah. I think I probably bought some tea or—

Reproduced with permission from *All-age Sketches for the Christian Year* published by BRF 2006 (1 84101 458 3)

www.barnabasinchurches.org.uk

Business: Invested in tea, eh? Can be quite risky. Import tariffs are crucial for the sustainability of price levels. *(Opens newspaper)* It says here, 'The recovery in the tea sector is as yet in its nascent stage. Investors should probably wait awhile before considering investments in tea stocks.' However, tea stocks have risen over the past week. (THINKS) So, if you invest a pound, that's... *(Gets out a calculator)* You should have made around 3.678 pence. Not bad.

Homeless: Sorry, you don't seem to get it. I just bought a cup of tea—

Business: Oh, so you purchased a tea for a pound, and sold it on for...?

Homeless: I just drank it. I needed warming up and—

Business: That was an asset. Your only asset. And you just gulped it down. *(Shakes head)* Oh dear.

Homeless: I didn't expect you to come back and demand a progress report. I thought you just gave me the pound—

Business: A gift? You thought—

Homeless: If you want the pound back... *(Grabs pound from pot, offers to BUSINESS)* here you are.

Business: You don't owe me a pound.

Homeless: Fine. *(Pops it back in pot)*

Business: You owe me one pound twenty.

Homeless: You what?

Reproduced with permission from *All-age Sketches for the Christian Year* published by BRF 2006 (1 84101 458 3)
www.barnabasinchurches.org.uk

Business: Return on investment. Business is business. I loan you a pound and—

Homeless: Loan?

Business: Yes. Bit of capital. Help you back on your feet.

Homeless: But I haven't got one pound twenty.

Business: That's not my fault. You wasted it. Poured your only capital asset down your throat.

Homeless: But even if I had invested it, I'd have only made 3.678 pence. So I'd have...

Business: (*Calculates*) ... still owed me 16.322 pence.

Homeless: I'll give you the one pound twenty next week. If I have it.

Business: No, you won't. (*Calculates*) It'll be one pound forty-four next week.

Homeless: What if I haven't got it?

Business: (*Calculates*) Then it'll be one pound seventy-three the week after. Two pound and seven pence the week after that. You'd better watch out. It'll be two thousand six hundred and twenty-two pence after a year—

Homeless: You what?

Business: Don't worry. If it comes to that, I'll let you off the twenty-two pence.

Homeless: But that's ridiculous. It's only a pound.

Business: There's nothing 'only' about money. When does it stop being 'only'? A fiver? Ten pounds? A hundred? A thousand? A million?

Reproduced with permission from *All-age Sketches for the Christian Year* published by BRF 2006 (1 84101 458 3)

www.barnabasinchurches.org.uk

Homeless: I just need a bit of help.

Business: Hand-outs! Is that what you want? Make a business plan. Find something people want. Then buy it for less and sell it for more. It's the only way to make it in life.

Homeless: I am trying to help myself, but it's not that easy—

PASSER approaches, looks at sign, can't find the pot to put the pound in.

Passer: *(Showing pound)* Where do you want this?

Business: *(Grabs)* I'll have that, if you don't mind.

Passer: You don't need it. *(Grabs back)* I'm giving it to him.

Business: But he owes it to me.

Passer: How much does he owe?

Business: One pound and twenty new pence.

Passer: Oh, forget about it.

Business: Are you mad?

Passer: What's the point? You don't need it.

Business: But I... it's the principle.

Passer: Here's a new principle for you: let him off.

Business: But it's just the tip of the iceberg. Where will it all end? If I let him off, what about all the other people who owe me more? And what about everyone else? Why should I do

Reproduced with permission from *All-age Sketches for the Christian Year* published by BRF 2006 (1 84101 458 3)
www.barnabasinchurches.org.uk

it when no one else does?

Passer: Start small. Let him off. Then see what happens.

Business: (*Flustered*) Oh, I don't know. I—

Passer: You don't need one pound twenty!

Business: Not right now, but—

Passer: Let him off.

Business: Oh, very well. This is most unbusinesslike. (*To HOMELESS*) Debt cancelled. You don't owe me anything.

Homeless: Thanks very much.

Passer: That's that. (*Pops pound in pot*) Goodbye.

Homeless: Cheers. And God bless.

Passer: And you.

PASSER leaves. BUSINESS is left rather flummoxed.

Business: (*Calculates*) I had a pound… I gave him a pound… he owed me a pound… I let him off the pound. So that's one pound. Minus a pound. Plus a pound. Then minus a pound again.

Homeless: Are you OK?

Business: Nothing. Oh. It's nothing. I… er… I'm a little confused.

Homeless: I know a good remedy for that.

Business: What?

Reproduced with permission from *All-age Sketches for the Christian Year* published by BRF 2006 (1 84101 458 3)

www.barnabasinchurches.org.uk

Homeless: A nice cup of tea. I've got a couple of pounds. It's on me.

Business: Might as well. *(Looks at watch)* Looks like I've missed the Jubilee train.

Homeless: Actually, I think you've just got it.

* * * END * * *

Reproduced with permission from *All-age Sketches for the Christian Year* published by BRF 2006 (1 84101 458 3)
www.barnabasinchurches.org.uk

Up, up and away

Curtain up

Ascension Day is one of the four most important events in the Christian year. The celebration falls on a Thursday in May or very early June, depending on the date of Easter. It is always 40 days after Easter Day and ten days before Pentecost.

Bible backdrop

MARK 13:32–37; 16:19–20; LUKE 24:50–51; ACTS 1:1–11

The ascension marks the final meeting between the risen Jesus and his disciples. It was the day on which Jesus told his closest friends that he would be with them always, and promised the gift of the Holy Spirit before he was taken up into heaven. But that is not the end of the story. Ascension Day also celebrates the kingship of Jesus and looks forward to the time when he will return in majesty and power.

Sermon prompt

With Jesus' return in mind, this sketch focuses on Jesus' teaching on the second coming as a time unknown to anyone but God himself. If Jesus doesn't know the exact moment of his return, then we certainly cannot. Those who devote long hours to trying to puzzle out a timetable for the end of the world are wasting their time. The message is rather that we must be ready, and obedient to the command to tell everyone we meet the good news of Jesus Christ.

Cast

Three performers: ONE, TWO and THREE (all male or female). ONE and TWO are close consorts and are wildly over the top, gesticulating excessively and talking in a pompous tone of voice. THREE, a passing stranger, is much more calm and level-headed.

Staging: props, costumes and effects

There's nothing complicated in the stage set-up. Any space will do and there are no props. If possible, ONE and TWO should be dressed in some sort of robe (dressing-gowns are a good substitute) and should have big, long grey beards (as all 'wise' men do). In contrast, THREE should be dressed unobtrusively, such as in black (black trousers and top).

Up, up and away

Scene: Mount of Olives. ONE and TWO are excited.

One: It's incredible.

Two: Amazing!

One: One second he's chatting away and then...
Zooooom!

Two: *(Joining in)* Vooooom!

One: (BEAT) I think it was more of a zoooom than a
voooom.

Two: Either/or, I suppose. *(Chuckles)* Not like it
matters.

One: No. Not like it's important. Anyway, there he is,
having a bit of a natter when... ZOOOOM!
(BEAT) He's taken up!

Two: Gone!

One: Left!

Two: Departed!

One: *(Looks up)* Disappeared!

Two: *(Looks up)* Vanished!

One: (THINKS) Absent!

Two: (THINKS) Off somewhere!

*As ONE and TWO stare up into the sky, THREE arrives
and stares at them, puzzled.*

Reproduced with permission from *All-age Sketches for the Christian Year* published by BRF 2006 (1 84101 458 3)

www.barnabasinchurches.org.uk

Three: Why are you standing here looking into the sky?

One: Incredible!

Two: Amazing!

Three: *(Looks up)* Can't see anything myself…

One: That's 'cos he's gone.

Two: Departed. One second he's jabbering away and then—

One: Zoooom!

Two: Voooom!

One: Current eschatological thinking is divided as to whether it was a zoooom or a voooom.

Three: What was?

Two: The ascension!

One: Jesus taken up to heaven, then seated at the right hand of the Father. First a zoooom and then a pop—and he's gone!

Two: Are you sure it was a pop?

One: What else would it be?

Two: I think it would be more of a… *(Does a sucking sound.)* More of an implosion.

One: What's that?

Two: An explosion is when something is blown outwards. An implosion is when something is pulled inwards. Jesus' body was solid matter. So when he disappeared, he must have left a gap, and the surrounding air must have sucked

Reproduced with permission from *All-age Sketches for the Christian Year* published by BRF 2006 (1 84101 458 3)
www.barnabasinchurches.org.uk

inwards to fill the space—an implosion rather than an explosion.

One: Very clever, I'm sure. You've explained an explosion and an implosion. So what's a plosion?

Two: (THINKS) Umm...

Three: (*Interrupting*) That's quite an amazing thing. Did it happen here?

Two: Most biblical scholars would concur that it was here.

Three: When did this happen?

One: Years ago!

Two: Ages ago!

Three: So why are you here now?

One: Aha. You see, Jesus, in the same way that he popped off—

Two: Or (*Sucks*)-ed off.

One: He promised he's coming back.

Two: There will be a great roar—voooom!

One: Or, more likely, zoooom!

Two: And he'll be back!

Three: Oh, when will that be?

One: (*Winks*) No one knows!

Two: Jesus said, 'No one knows the day or the time. The angels in heaven don't know, and the Son himself doesn't know. Only the Father knows.'

One: But guess what?

Three: What?

Two: Can you keep a secret?

Three: Probably.

One: *(Excited)* Can we tell him?

Two: *(Excited)* Oh, go on!

One: The thing is... we reckon we've worked it out—when he's coming back!

Three: How did you work it out?

Two: *(Whispering)* Clues.

One: *(Whispering)* Secret clues.

Two: *(Whispering)* Hidden.

One: *(Whispering)* In the Bible.

Two: Daniel, Revelation, the Table of Weights and Measures... take a look, it's all there.

One: *(Taps nose)* If you know where to look for it...

Two: *(Taps nose)* ... and how to interpret it.

One: *(Whispering)* All the evidence points to the fact that we are currently living in the End Times.

Three: Does it?

Two: Haven't the time to go through all the details, but—

One: *(Serious)* Trust us.

Two: *(Nodding)* It's now.

Three: So when is Jesus coming back?

One: Ooh. Couldn't really say... *(Winks)* But it might be soon...

Three: How soon?

Two: No one knows the day or time. But it might be—

One: (*Excited*) In about two minutes' time!

Three: You what? How do you know?

Two: Calculations...

One: Research...

Two: Reading... a lot.

Three: How long have you known?

One: Ages... but we've been busy.

Two: Checking the facts.

Three: Shouldn't you be out there telling people?

One: I said, we've been busy!

Two: Do you think it's easy to discover hidden secrets like that?

One: It's taken years of study...

Two: Poring over old books...

One: Examining the original text and meaning...

Two: Doing really difficult sums...

Three: But if Jesus said no one would know the day—

One: Hey! (*Looks up*) It should be starting about now.

Three: What's starting?

Two: Jesus himself will come down from heaven, with a loud command...

One: With the voice of the archangel and with the trumpet call of God...

Reproduced with permission from *All-age Sketches for the Christian Year* published by BRF 2006 (1 84101 458 3)
www.barnabasinchurches.org.uk

Two: And the dead in Christ will rise first.

One: After that, we who are still alive and are left will be caught up together with them in the clouds to meet the Lord in the air.

Two: And so we will be with the Lord for ever.

One: We should start to rise any second now!

Two: (*Serious*) Hang on. (*Gulps*) I can feel something...

One: Can you?

Three: What is it?

Two: Something rising up inside!

One: That's not fair! What about me?

Two: (*Clutches his chest*) I think something's happening... (*Raises his arms*) I can feel something welling up... (BEAT. *ONE and THREE stare at TWO expectantly. TWO burps loudly.* BEAT) Oh. I think it was a bit of trapped wind.

Three: Hmm. Yes. You both seem rather full of hot air.

One: (*Long pause*) Looks like it's not today, then.

Two: But it was worth coming, you know, just in case.

Three: Is this what you are supposed to be doing— hanging, about waiting for Jesus?

One: What else should we do?

Three: What did Jesus say before he left: 'Won't be a tick, wait here—I'll be back soon'?

Two: No, idiot. The last thing he said was, 'The Holy Spirit will come upon you and give you power.

Reproduced with permission from *All-age Sketches for the Christian Year* published by BRF 2006 (1 84101 458 3)
www.barnabasinchurches.org.uk

Then you will tell everyone about me in Jerusalem, in all Judea, in Samaria, and everywhere in the world.' Everyone knows that.

Three: Then shouldn't you be doing that?

One: *(Sudden revelation)* Yes. Of course. I've got it!

Two: What?

One: We've got our sums wrong!

Two: But I checked it thoroughly!

One: We're 33 years out!

Two: You don't mean…?

One: We calculated it from Jesus' birth, not his death!

Two: You're right!

One: Back to the books! We've another 33 years to finish our studies.

Three: But this is stupid!

Two: Come back here in 33 years' time and we'll show you stupid!

One: Just don't tell anyone else.

Two: Unless they can keep a secret.

One: I can't wait. Zoooom! Pop!

Two: Don't you mean voooom… *(Sucks)*?

They exit.

* * * END * * *

Gone with the wind

Curtain up

Pentecost is the festival when Christians celebrate the gift of the Holy Spirit. It is celebrated on the Sunday 50 days after Easter and can fall in either May or June, depending on the date of Easter. Pentecost is regarded as the birthday of the Christian Church, and the start of the Church's mission to the world.

Bible backdrop

ACTS 2:1–41

The Day of Pentecost began with 'a noise from heaven like the sound of a mighty wind'. Then, 'what looked like fiery tongues' came and settled on each person in the house where the disciples were meeting. As with the resurrection, the events of Pentecost can be helped by a fresh perspective to understand fully the unexpected impact. So strange were the events and the behaviour of the apostles that the Bible records how some observers made fun of the spectacle, claiming that Jesus' followers were drunk and disorderly.

Sermon prompt

This sketch takes up the story from the moment of the arrival of the Holy Spirit, concentrating on Peter, who has literally been through a whirlwind and discovered a new calling far beyond his humble background as a fisherman. As the sketch centres on Peter, it could also be used during a series about his life or the early church.

Cast

Three performers: SARGE and CONSTABLE (male or female) represent the local Roman authorities, but they are characterized as modern-day police officers. The third character, PETER (male), is still on a bit of a high from the events of the day.

Staging: props, costumes and effects

The set is a police interview room, so the addition of a classic bright spotlight lamp would be a useful, if anachronistic, signifier. For the costumes, you can make the police either Roman guards or modern-day police officers, either of which will require a trip to the fancy-dress shop. If you are on a budget, a couple of kids' police helmets would be a good purchase (and useful in general for drama). PETER can either be in stereotypical biblical character costume—robes, sandals and a beard—or in everyday clothes for a modern twist.

Props include a set of keys for PETER (big comedy ones if possible), a pen and pad, and a few sheets of paper (witness statements) for CONSTABLE. A cock crows at one point, so either use a sound effect or get someone to perform it on cue.

Gone with the wind

Scene: A police interrogation room. SARGE is sitting behind a desk next to a chair. Opposite is a chair for the prisoner, PETER.

Sarge: Bring in the disgusting specimen, Constable. (*CONSTABLE leads PETER in*) Sore head?

Peter: I'm afraid this is all a complete misunderstanding—

Sarge: I'd be surprised if you haven't got one after what you've allegedly been up to today. Have you got a sore head?

Peter: No. It's fine.

Constable: (*Threatening*) Would you like one?

Sarge: Basic interrogation first, Constable. Advanced interrogation later—if you are a good boy.

Peter: Oh, I will be.

Sarge: Not you, reprobate. You definitely won't enjoy the advanced interrogation.

Peter: Best get this little mistake cleared up then, eh?

Sarge: You realize these are very serious accusations—

Peter: I know that, but—

Constable: (*Shouting*) Name?

Reproduced with permission from *All-age Sketches for the Christian Year* published by BRF 2006 (1 84101 458 3)
www.barnabasinchurches.org.uk

Peter: Oh. That's rather complicated—

Sarge: I know you. It's Simon, isn't it?

Peter: Simon or Peter—

Constable: Which is it?

Peter: Either. I mean neither. I mean both.

Sarge: *(Dictating)* Prisoner appeared to be in a confused state. He did not know his own name—

Peter: Of course I do. But... the thing is—

Constable: Occupation?

Peter: I'm the leader of the twelve disciples. I mean, apostles—

Constable: Which is it?

Peter: Apostles now. Sorry. We changed it recently.

Constable: *(Impatient)* What is your occupation?

Peter: I'm sorry, things have been a bit strange today. I've just sort of discovered—or was given, really—a new calling today. I'm a preacher. Evangelist. But I suppose you'd say I'm really the leader of a new Jewish sect.

Sarge: Next thing, you'll be telling us you're the Bishop of Rome.

SARGE and CONSTABLE laugh.

Constable: What's the name of this 'sect'?

Peter: We haven't really got around to having a name yet. We've toyed with a few ideas. The Jesusians? The Christofollowers? Or the Messianiacs on the loose? That one was Simon the Zealot's idea—he's a bit excitable.

Sarge: *(Dictating)* Prisoner seemed delirious, babbling away like a fool.

Peter: We do have a 'naming ourselves' sub-committee. Thomas is in charge, but he doubts he'll come up with anything—

Constable: What shall I put as your occupation? And keep it simple.

Peter: (THINKS) Fisherman?

Sarge: *(Dictating)* Prisoner appeared to be unaware of the seriousness of the charges against him.

Peter: I am fully aware of the serious accusations.

Sarge: Do you admit the charges?

Peter: No, I do not.

Sarge: Are you sure?

Peter: Perfectly!

Sarge: I'll give you one last chance. Did you do it?

Peter: No, absolutely not. *(A cock crows)* What is it with that bird? It's got it in for me! But I'm telling the truth this time.

Sarge: You are accused of being drunk and disorderly in a public place. Admit it! You made a public spectacle of yourself after

Reproduced with permission from *All-age Sketches for the Christian Year* published by BRF 2006 (1 84101 458 3)
www.barnabasinchurches.org.uk

consuming copious quantities of cheap wine.

Peter: But that's simply not true!

Constable: Can you, then, give a full account of the events of this morning in your own words?

Peter: Thank you. Yes. The disciples—

Sarge: Apostles?

Peter: Yes. I'm not quite used to it yet, but the apostles, the eleven—

Sarge: Twelve?

Peter: Sorry. We've just voted in a new member. The twelve of us met together—

Sarge: Social gathering, was it?

Peter: How do you mean?

Constable: Did you consume anything?

Peter: That's not really the point—

Constable: For the record, sir?

Peter: OK. We had a bit of dinner. Bartholomew makes a delightful spicy bean casserole—

Sarge: Anything... *(Coughs)* else?

Peter: Yes, we had a Prune Surprise to follow. Then suddenly we experienced this mighty wind—

Sarge: I'm not surprised after what you'd eaten.

Peter: No. It was like a tornado. It filled the whole room.

Constable: You should have opened a window.

Reproduced with permission from *All-age Sketches for the Christian Year* published by BRF 2006 (1 84101 458 3)

www.barnabasinchurches.org.uk

Peter: *(Ignoring them. Excited)* Then—like wildfire—it came! Then it separated and came to rest on each of us!

Constable: What was 'it'?

Peter: It was… some kind of spirit—

Sarge: Spirits, eh? Note that down, Constable.

Constable: *(Writing)* Gathered apostles consumed spirits.

Peter: You're not listening. *(Continues)* I could feel this burning sensation!

Sarge: I don't know how you reprobates drink that cheap plonk!

Peter: Then these people came to us. A crowd, out of nowhere, gathered round us—amazed!

Sarge: People shouldn't encourage drunkards like you. I've heard enough. Read from the witness statements, Constable. Now we'll hear the truth.

Constable: *(Rummages through papers)* Here it is: 'The strange group of glowing men started to speak in Mesopotamian…' *(Stops)* Oh, that's odd. *(Swaps paper)* This one says, 'The fiery bunch of blokes began to babble in the Parthian tongue.' *(Frowns)* But then this one says they spoke in Arabic. And this one says they were shouting in Egyptian. But in this one it's Libyan—

Sarge: Can't we, for once, get some consistent witnesses? Cretins! They're all cretins!

Reproduced with permission from *All-age Sketches for the Christian Year* published by BRF 2006 (1 84101 458 3)
www.barnabasinchurches.org.uk

Constable: No, only this one. Christopher from Crete, who says—

Sarge: Shut up. (*Turns to PETER*) Did you have anything to drink this morning?

Peter: I had a drop of wine—just a sip.

Sarge: A sip?

Peter: It's one of our new rituals. We're thinking about calling it wineshare or bloodsipping or togethertime. I'm sure we'll think of a better name. But it's not really about the alcohol. It's something Jesus taught us to do. The wine changes into his blood or symbolizes his blood—anyway, it doesn't really matter, the point is—

Sarge: (*Shouting*) Stop jabbering! (BEAT) It seems, Simon (*Correcting*) Peter, or whatever your name is, we can't find any evidence against you. You are free to go and preach, or lead the disciples—I mean apostles—or fish, or whatever it is that you do. Just get out of my sight!

Peter: You're letting me go free? Just wait until I tell Thomas. He'll never believe me! Thanks for everything!

Constable: Just one moment, sir.

Peter: Yes?

Constable: (*Producing keys*) Your keys?

Reproduced with permission from *All-age Sketches for the Christian Year* published by BRF 2006 (1 84101 458 3)

www.barnabasinchurches.org.uk

Peter: Oops! Better not forget those! *(As he exits)* Wow! What an eventful day. Must think of a name for it. Spiritday? Translationevent? Windcoming? Oh, I'm sure we'll think of something more memorable. Something in Latin perhaps—always lends a bit of gravitas...

* * * END * * *

Reproduced with permission from *All-age Sketches for the Christian Year* published by BRF 2006 (1 84101 458 3)
www.barnabasinchurches.org.uk

130

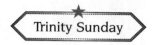
Three become one

Curtain up

Trinity Sunday falls on the first Sunday after Pentecost and is observed as one of the principal feasts in the Christian year.

Bible backdrop

MATTHEW 28:19; ROMANS 1:1–4

The word 'Trinity' describes the biblical concept of who God is, the evidence of which is especially recorded in the New Testament. Trinity Sunday is the celebration of the threefold nature of God (Father, Son and Holy Spirit) and marks the revelation of all three persons of the Godhead after the festival of Pentecost.

Sermon prompt

Quite a lot is made of the complexity of the theory of the Trinity—how difficult it is to understand and how much study is required to grasp it fully as a theological concept. This is, of course, nonsense. The Trinity can be understood by anyone—children, people with little education or university professors—and this sketch explains how. For this reason, it is also a sketch about how Christianity is something that can be understood by everyone, and just because you have studied a lot, it doesn't mean you are closer to God's heart.

Of course, this is not to say that the Trinity is a 'simple' concept. None of us will be able to explain it fully this side of heaven, but we do know enough to trust and accept that God is three persons, as well as being one God.

Cast

Two performers: ONE and TWO (both male or female). TWO is on stage for the whole sketch, whereas ONE exits and enters a number of times. ONE will need a large book and a stack of printed paper.

Staging: props, costumes and effects

There is no set to speak of, and ONE and TWO can wear everyday clothes. If you want to give them costumes, make ONE appear to be an intellectual and TWO more down to earth.

This sketch is reliant upon the possession of three props: a three-legged stool, a musical triangle and a packet of Jaffa Cakes. The latter can be passed round at the end of the sketch (or shared by the cast if you're not feeling too generous).

Three become one

Scene: On stage is a stool. A fraught and serious ONE is pacing up and down, deep in thought. The jovial and laid-back TWO enters and looks at ONE inquisitively.

One: *(Thinking aloud)* Trinity... tri-nity... tri-ni-ty!

Two: Are you OK?

One: *(Ignoring ONE, deep in concentration)* It's three but it's also one. But it's three as well, and one at the same time. But while it is one, it is also three.

Two: Can I help?

One: *(Dismissive)* I don't think so, do you? I am attempting to grasp a complex theological concept. I don't believe a useless, lazy, brainless lump like you could possibly help.

Two: *(Not bothered)* What are you trying to understand?

One: I really don't think— *(Sighs)* Oh, very well. Anything to spare me your idiotic inquiries. I am attempting to learn about the Trinity.

Two: The Trinity? God in three persons, Father, Son and Holy Spirit?

One: Dear, oh dear! It's not as simple as that, is it? How can three be one. And one be three. And be one. All at the same time. As well as being three?

Two: Sounds interesting. What does the word 'Trinity' mean?

Reproduced with permission from *All-age Sketches for the Christian Year* published by BRF 2006 (1 84101 458 3)

www.barnabasinchurches.org.uk

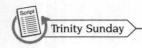

One: If you break it down, 'tri' means three, as in tricycle. Then there's 'nity', which is... er... (THINKS) 'nity' is...

Two: ... what you call someone who has nits?

One: I knew you wouldn't help matters. I shall consult my vast library of theological texts, where I'm sure to find the answer. (BEAT) What are you going to do?

Two: I might just have a little sit-down on this stool.

One: Pathetic! Whilst you are sat on your bottom, I shall be examining one of the great mysteries that has baffled scholars for two thousand years. I shall return enlightened!

ONE exits. TWO sits on the stool, thinking for a short while. ONE returns, holding a book.

One: Eureka!

Two: Do you have an answer?

One: No, but I have stumbled upon a tome which will help me with my studies.

Two: What's it called?

One: *An Eschatological Examination of the Trinity Using Hermeneutics and Exegesis.*

Two: How far have you got?

One: I'm still grappling with the title...

Two: Doesn't sound much like progress.

Reproduced with permission from *All-age Sketches for the Christian Year* published by BRF 2006 (1 84101 458 3)
www.barnabasinchurches.org.uk

One: It's better than sitting about doing nothing!

Two: I haven't been doing nothing. I've been thinking.

One: No wonder you've had to rest on that stool.

Two: It's interesting, this stool. It has three legs.

One: Good job, otherwise you'd have fallen off.

Two: Precisely. If it only had one leg, or even two legs, it would be useless. It's the perfect number of legs for a stool—

One: Sorry, but I can't stay here all day talking about furniture. The mystery of the Trinity must be unravelled. I shall return to my studies…

ONE exits. TWO produces a triangle and begins to play. Shortly, ONE returns.

One: Please can you cut out that racket! I am trying to think!

Two: *(Stops playing)* Sorry. How's it going?

One: Brilliant. Excellent. Marvellous! (BEAT) Actually, not very well… I've abandoned the book. It was obviously written by a lesser intellect than myself, who has an inability to grasp certain basic fundamental principles. For that reason, I was unable to comprehend a single word of it…

Two: Sounds like you're back to square one.

One: That's one square better than you! At least I'm trying to understand, rather than just sitting around creating a dreadful cacophony!

Reproduced with permission from *All-age Sketches for the Christian Year* published by BRF 2006 (1 84101 458 3)

www.barnabasinchurches.org.uk

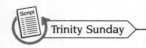

Two: It's interesting, this triangle. Each of the three sides works in harmony with the others. Take one away and the instrument wouldn't work—

One: Stop distracting me with your nonsense! I am on a quest to find an answer, and we all know where you can discover the truth, the whole truth and nothing but the truth.

Two: Where's that?

One: The Internet! I shall surf the vast knowledge of billions of people across the globe to find an answer. (BEAT) What are you going to do?

Two: I'm feeling a bit peckish, actually…

One: I'll leave you to stuff your face, while I shall feast on knowledge!

ONE exits. TWO opens a packet of Jaffa Cakes and begins eating. Shortly, ONE returns with a massive print-out of paper.

One: *(Exasperated)* There are over six million results when you search for 'trinity' on the Internet! There's Trinity colleges, universities, churches…

Two: What does that mean?

One: It means that I'll have to spend weeks trawling through this lot if I want to understand anything about the Trinity! I give up!

Two: Would you like a Jaffa Cake?

One: Oh, go on, then. I suppose it can't make things worse. *(TWO gives ONE a Jaffa Cake)*

Reproduced with permission from *All-age Sketches for the Christian Year* published by BRF 2006 (1 84101 458 3)
www.barnabasinchurches.org.uk

Two: Interesting things, Jaffa Cakes. There's three parts: a chocolatey top; a cakey, biscuity part underneath; and an orangey jam section in the middle. Each part has an individual flavour, distinctive and delicious in its own way. But put them together and it's even better.

One: *(Fed up)* I feel like I've learned more about stools, triangles and Jaffa Cakes today than the Trinity.

Two: Really?

One: *(Suddenly enlightened)* Just a minute! You fool! Don't you see?

Two: What?

One: Each of these things does tell us about the Trinity! The stool tells us that the Trinity has three parts, or pillars, that provide support—and you need all three to have a stable foundation! The triangle tells us that the three parts work together to create harmony—a unity. And the Jaffa Cake tells us that each part, the Father, Son and Holy Spirit, is unique, distinct and has its own flavour—but put them together and you have something better, a greater whole!

Two: Or a tasty snack. *(Munching cake)* Interesting, isn't it?

One: I knew I would discover the answer! While you've been sat here, making a racket and stuffing your face, I've uncovered three simple ways to understand a complex theological concept. Three ways of looking at one thing! I am indeed a

Reproduced with permission from *All-age Sketches for the Christian Year* published by BRF 2006 (1 84101 458 3)

www.barnabasinchurches.org.uk

genius! *(Smug)* I shall leave you now. My work here is done. (BEAT) Don't worry, there's no need to thank me!

ONE exits. TWO finishes his mouthful.

Two: That's all right. I won't.

* * * END * * *

No such thing as a free supper

Curtain up

Corpus Christi is the day of thanksgiving for the institution of Holy Communion. The festival falls on the Thursday after Trinity Sunday, ten days after Pentecost. However, as Holy Communion is a regular occurrence, the sketch could be used at other times. It is also appropriate for Maundy Thursday, which marks the occasion of the Lord's Supper.

Bible backdrop

LUKE 22:1–23; JOHN 13:1–17

Corpus Christi literally means 'the body of Christ'. In the second or third century, the early (persecuted) church was accused by the Roman authorities of, among other things, cannibalism. It's easy to see where the notion came from: whispers of secret ceremonies where the followers of Jesus have a feast and claim to eat his flesh and drink his blood.

Sermon prompt

From an outside point of view, the sacrament of Holy Communion is a bit strange, and that's exactly what we witness in this sketch. It's the very first celebration of Holy Communion, seen from an outside perspective: that of the owners of the upper room where Jesus and his disciples gathered. It also narrates the other 'odd' things that

Jesus did at his last meal: having supper with a man he knew would betray him, and washing his disciples' feet.

Cast

Two performers: OWNER and WAITER (male or female). It is probable historically that the OWNER would have been a man and the person serving would have been a woman.

Staging: props, costumes and effects

There's not much in the way of a set, but a few props are needed, including a large water jar, a tray with some scraps of bread on it and a wine goblet containing a drop of wine. At the end of the sketch the wine goblet is smashed, so take a visit to a charity shop and make sure the breakage is done safely (clay is less dangerous than glass when smashed).

No such thing as a free supper

Scene: WAITER enters, carrying a water jar and tray.
The tray holds a cup and a plate with a few crumbs of bread
on it.

Owner: Put that water jar down. It's caused enough problems for one night.

Waiter: You can't blame the jar.

Owner: I know. I must have gone loopy.

Waiter: Yeah. We'd just spent all day sweeping, dusting and scrubbing, making the upper room all tidy. Then you unexpectedly agreed to lay on a feast for 13 complete strangers. What happened?

Owner: I have no idea. You arrived back from the well, saying these two blokes had followed you home. Thanks to that jar—

Waiter: I said, don't blame the jar. They told me they wanted to speak to the owner. What did they say to you?

Owner: They asked where the guest room was, and was it OK if they had their Passover meal there.

Waiter: And you thought: 'Great, a dozen strangers have turned up unexpectedly after following a large water jar. I know, I'll invite them all in for a massive feast—'

Owner: But they said that 'The Master' had sent them. 'The Master', see?

Waiter: What Master? Do you know him?

Owner: No. But he sounds terribly important, don't you think? Some sort of teacher, rabbi or other. Could be good for trade—get some classier clientele. You never know, he might become a regular customer.

Waiter: I don't think so. Not after what I've just heard.

Owner: What?

Waiter: As I went in to top up the drinks, this Master fellow declared that he was going to be arrested. And that one of his mates was going to do the dirty on him. Turn him in to the authorities.

Owner: You what? And he was having a cosy supper with this bloke? Knowing what he was about to do?

Waiter: If you think that's weird, I haven't told you what went on before that—

Owner: Go on—

Waiter: Earlier on in the evening, this Master fellow suddenly stood up, just as they were tucking into their lamb cutlets, and stripped down to his towel.

Owner: During dinner?

Waiter: Seemed a bit strange to me. Then he asked me for the water jar—

Reproduced with permission from *All-age Sketches for the Christian Year* published by BRF 2006 (1 84101 458 3)
www.barnabasinchurches.org.uk

Owner: I knew the jar had something to do with it! What did he want it for?

Waiter: His followers got quite excited. I think they thought he was going to turn the water into wine. But he didn't. He poured it into a bowl. Then he started going round all his mates and washing their feet.

Owner: I thought he was the boss of the outfit?

Waiter: Yeah. They were all looking confused, too. One of them started arguing about who's gonna wash whose feet. This other chap wanted to wash the Master's feet. But he wasn't having any of it. The Master then put his robe back on, sat back at the table, and the meal started over again. Just as things seemed back to normal, that's when he declared that one of them was about to hand him over to the authorities. Then they all got into a kerfuffle about that. They started saying, 'It's not me. Who is it? Is it him?'

Owner: What happened then?

Waiter: Unfortunately, I had to pop out to collect more water. But... (*Looks over his shoulder*) as I was going back, one of them rushed past me in the corridor. (*Whispering*) Shifty-looking fellow, clutching a bit of recently dipped bread. (*Winks*)

Owner: (*Whispering*) And that means?

Waiter: No idea. But he was off somewhere in a hurry. *(Taps his nose)*

Owner: I hope the rest of the meal passed without incident.

Waiter: It gets stranger.

Owner: Oh dear.

Waiter: The Master picks up the bread and breaks it. Then passes it round for everyone to eat.

Owner: Sounds relatively normal.

Waiter: Apart from the fact that, before doing it, he said, 'This is my body, which is given for you. Eat this as a way of remembering me!'

Owner: That's weird. Was he saying the bread tasted off? I baked it this afternoon...

Waiter: Here's some crumbs left over from the Master's table. *(Offers a bit)* Try some.

Owner: *(Eats bread)* Tastes all right. You try some. *(Offers bread to WAITER, who takes it)*

Waiter: Nothing unusual about it. Then again—

Owner: 'Eat this as a way of remembering me!' Strange thing to say.

Waiter: Yeah. Makes it sound like he doesn't expect to be around much longer. And after supper, he did another strange thing. *(Picks up the goblet)* He took this cup and said, 'This is my blood.'

Owner: Yuck! It's enough to put you off. (*Takes a sip*) Tastes fine. It's new wine, that. What was he thinking?

Waiter: After he said, 'This is my blood', he carried on, 'With it God makes a new agreement.'

Owner: (*Sarcastic*) Oh. That explains it, then.

Waiter: And there was something even more strange about it. This Master, he really seemed to believe it all. And his followers, they believed it. But—strangest of all—I believed it, too. (*Takes a sip of wine*)

Owner: Give that here. You're off your head. (*Grabs at the goblet and knocks it out of WAITER's hands. It smashes*) Bother! Clear this mess up. It's been an expensive waste of an evening. Thanks to that jar! (*Points to the jar*)

Waiter: Don't blame the jar. I tell you what. (*Bending over, picking up pieces*) The cup's not too badly broken. I'll collect up all the pieces and fix it.

Owner: What's the point? Just throw it in the bin. It's not like anyone's gonna come looking for it. (*Storms off*)

* * * END * * *

Reproduced with permission from *All-age Sketches for the Christian Year* published by BRF 2006 (1 84101 458 3)

www.barnabasinchurches.org.uk

Fathers Anonymous

Curtain up

Father's Day is celebrated on the third Sunday in June. Although Father's Day is not a traditional festival of the Christian year, it is included here as it is widely celebrated and is a good time to consider the role of fathers, and the father-heart of God.

The sketch could also be used as part of a parenting course or in a series about God as a father. However, because of the sensitive subject matter, it would be wise to prepare people to help with pastoral care for fathers or other men and women who identify with the sketch.

Bible backdrop

MARK 1:11

'You are my own dear Son, and I am pleased with you': this was the moment when God could contain his silence no longer. It is an outburst; an outpouring of love and pride from God, spoken out directly and publicly to his Son when heaven is torn open and the Holy Spirit, in the form of a dove, is seen coming down upon Jesus in affirmation of his identity and his ministry.

Sermon prompt

Sadly, some fathers do not directly declare their love for their sons or daughters. While I can't say exactly why this is the case, I am sure it is not because they do not possess those feelings. It may be a historical thing, it may be a pride thing, it could be anything. But I'm sure of one thing: it's not a good thing.

This sketch is about a group of fathers who keep their feelings hidden because they believe it is the right thing to do. They consider that their sons should grit their teeth and face the world, tough and strong. But silencing their feelings does not have the desired effect for their offspring or themselves.

Cast

Four performers: TED (male) is the group leader; PHIL and SAM (both male) are long-term members of the group. PHIL is about 20 years older than SAM. TOM (male) is new to the group. He is younger than the others, but only slightly younger than SAM.

Staging: props, costumes and effects

Very simple stage set-up: a few tatty chairs set out in a semicircle. All four characters have a grotty cup of tea in a plastic cup. They wear everyday modern clothes.

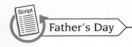

Fathers Anonymous

Scene: Four men of various ages are sitting in a semicircle drinking weak tea and munching on stale biscuits. On the edge is TOM, who is clearly new. In the centre is TED, their leader.

Ted: (*Rising*) Thank you all for coming out on a Saturday morning. I hope you all find the new time and day more convenient for avoiding the... (*Whispers*) unmentionables. We'll start in the usual fashion. (BEAT. *TED presents himself*) My name is Ted and I've been a... (*Looks over shoulder*) you-know-what for 15 years. (*The rest of the group clap feebly. TED sits*)

Phil: (*Rises*) My name is Phil and I've been a... (*Whispers*) one of them... for 26 years. (*Sits as group applauds*)

Sam: (*Rises*) My name is Sam and I've also been a... (*Looks around*) what he didn't say... for three years. (*Sits as group applauds*)

Ted: Well done, group. We stick together, and we'll get through this... (*Bites lip*) together. Now, you may have noticed we have a new member: (*Indicates*) Tom. You can tell by the worried expression, the pallid complexion, the bags under his eyes, and the weight on his shoulders that he's... (*Leans forward*) one of us. (*Group pat TOM in a manly fashion on the back*)

Reproduced with permission from *All-age Sketches for the Christian Year* published by BRF 2006 (1 84101 458 3)
www.barnabasinchurches.org.uk

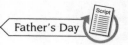
Phil: We know how it feels, mate.

Sam: Good on yer.

Ted: Can you introduce yourself, lad?

Tom: *(Cheery)* I'm Tom and I've just become a father—

Group gasps. PAUSE.

Sam: We don't use the F-word here.

Tom: Sorry. I… er… didn't know. (THINKS) How about if I use the word 'dad'?

Phil: Terrible!

Tom: 'Daddy'?

Sam: *(Screams)* Worse.

Ted: It's all right, everyone, let's stay focused. He's new to the group. *(To TOM)* Tom. If you must refer to your… *(Whispers)* parental *(SAM and PHIL shudder)* position, please use the phrase 'you-know-what'. Or some other euphemism—just don't use any of the words you've just said.

Tom: OK. But I don't see— *(TED shakes his head; TOM resigns himself)* My name's Tom and I've just— well, only last week actually—become a… (THINKS) You know, the thing I'm not supposed to— *(Group applauds)*

Ted: Well done, Tom. It's going to be a long, hard, painful road ahead. But don't fret. We—the group—will be here to share the hard times, the difficult times, the painful times, the rotten times,

Reproduced with permission from *All-age Sketches for the Christian Year* published by BRF 2006 (1 84101 458 3)

www.barnabasinchurches.org.uk

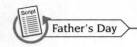

and, of course, the miserable times. When it gets bad—and it will—we will be here to share the agony. And I tell you, if you think it's dreadful now, believe me, it will get a hell of a lot worse. (BEAT) Sam, I believe it's your turn to share something about your struggles from this week.

Sam: This week? *(Worried)* It's been bad, Ted. Very bad.

Ted: Come on. *(Cheery but sinister)* You can tell us…

Sam: I did an awful thing.

Phil: What kind of thing?

Sam: I told someone my… feelings.

Ted: *(Deadpan)* What kind of feelings, Sam?

Sam: I just came out with it. I don't know what was the matter with me—

Ted: *(Stern)* What did you say?

Sam: I said. Out loud. That I'm proud of him.

Tom: Proud of who?

Sam: My… my… *(Gulps)* I said I was proud of my son. *(Bursts into tears)*

Phil: *(Solemn)* Oh dear. Oh dear.

Tom: But surely—?

Ted: *(Stern)* Now, come on, Sam. Buck your ideas up a bit. When did 'emotion' ever solve anything? You know what to do. Repress it. Repress it. Come on. Bury it deep down inside. Deep. Deep. Down. (BEAT) Have you buried it? *(SAM nods)* Does it still hurt?

Reproduced with permission from *All-age Sketches for the Christian Year* published by BRF 2006 (1 84101 458 3)
www.barnabasinchurches.org.uk

Sam: Yes.

Ted: But you'll put a brave face on it?

Sam: *(Bucking himself up)* That's right, Ted. Fine and dandy now. *(Smiles unconvincingly)* Great.

Tom: Can I ask a question?

Ted: Not just now, Tom. *(Turns to SAM)* Right. About this unfortunate emotional outburst. Was it in public?

Sam: I'm afraid so.

Ted: Oh dear. Who did you tell? Not your unmentionable?

Sam: No, thank goodness. I told the landlord of the Dog and Duck. *(Shakes head)* I'm sorry. I've let everyone down. I'd had one too many and I couldn't help myself…

Ted: Is it your local?

Sam: No. It's miles away. Thank goodness.

Ted: So they don't know you?

Sam: No. I was just there for the evening.

Ted: OK. That's good. You must never go there again. And with a bit of luck, no one will ever know it was you.

Sam: I promise I'll never do anything so stupid again.

Ted: You have said that before, Sam. Now, I don't mean to dig up the past—

Tom: *(Interrupting)* Excuse me? Sorry. But I don't understand. Sam, did you say that you were proud of your son?

Phil: Don't say it again. And keep your voice down!

Tom: What's wrong with saying you are... what he said... of your... um, unmentionable?

Ted: Oh dear. (*Chuckles*) You have got a lot to learn.

Tom: But surely... I mean. I'm sure there can be frustrations in being a you-know-what. But isn't it natural to say nice things about your... offspring? (*PHIL and SAM groan*)

Ted: I can see you are going to be difficult, Tom. (BEAT) No, it is not natural. No, it is not good. No, it is not right. (*Nods*) Tell him, Phil.

Phil: We're here because we want our...

Sam: We want them to grow up right...

Phil: Teach them to be strong...

Sam: Face the world...

Phil: Stand up straight...

Sam: On their own two feet...

Phil: Pull their socks up...

Sam: Stick their finger out...

Tom: But surely—?

Ted: We don't want the little tykes to grow up to be mollycoddled, lily-livered softies who have to be wrapped up in cotton wool with silver spoons in their mouths! We want to send them to the school of hard knocks, put them through the university of life, and out into the rat race—where it's dog-eat-dog!

Reproduced with permission from *All-age Sketches for the Christian Year* published by BRF 2006 (1 84101 458 3)
www.barnabasinchurches.org.uk

Tom: But wouldn't they be better suited to getting through life with some support? *(Group gasps)* Some affection? *(More gasps)* Encouragement? *(Bigger gasps)* Affirmation? *(Biggest gasps)* And love? *(The group is speechless)*

Ted: *(Jittery)* Right. *(Points)* You. Listen. You. This is my class—

Tom: Don't you love your children? Phil? Sam?

PHIL and SAM look to TED.

Ted: Well, of course we… *(Gestures)* what you said. But we don't want to tell them that…

Tom: But why not? Phil? Don't you ever want to tell your… *(PHIL turns away, arms folded)* Sam, didn't your dad ever say that he loved you?

Sam: *(Bursts into tears)* No. He's never said it. *(Shaking his fists in the air)* Why? Why? Why did you never say it, Daddy? Why?

PAUSE.

Phil: Because he told me not to. *(Indicates TED)* That's why. Ted told me it would do you good.

Ted: And it has. It's made him the man he is today. *(SAM blows his nose loudly between sobs)*

Tom: Well, it's never too late in my book. Come on, Phil. Tell him. *(PHIL looks at TED)* Except, of course, if you don't love him…

Reproduced with permission from *All-age Sketches for the Christian Year* published by BRF 2006 (1 84101 458 3)

www.barnabasinchurches.org.uk

Phil: But of course I... *(Turns to SAM. Takes a deep breath)* I love you, sonny boy.

Sam: Me too, Pops. *(They hug. TED looks on, his lip quivering)*

Tom: Are you OK, Ted?

Ted: Yeah. I've just got... *(Holding back the tears)* something in my eye. (BEAT) Must be someone chopping onions in the cookery class along the corridor. If you'll excuse me, I've got something to do. Some bridges to build. *(He exits swiftly)*

Tom: Should I go after him?

Phil: It's OK, he'll be fine.

Tom: Sounds promising, though: 'bridges to build'.

Sam: That's right. His son's in a bridge construction class next door.

* * * END * * *

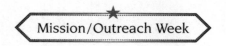

Knock, knock, knocking

Curtain up

In response to Jesus' call to his followers to proclaim the gospel, the mission of the church is ongoing and broad-based. However, many churches set a week aside specifically to reach out to people within the local community, usually around the summer holidays in July or August. Having said that, this sketch is suitable for use all the year round—any time when your church needs to be inspired and reminded that the harvest is ripe and that we few workers should be out there reaping.

Bible backdrop

LUKE 5:1–11; 9:1–6; 10:1–12; 1 PETER 3:15

Telling others the good news of the kingdom of God is not an occupation for those who seek personal comfort and security. Many are unwilling to hear, while others are full of disdain and mistrust. However, Jesus chose his first four disciples in order for them to bring in people instead of fish. He selected the Twelve to proclaim the good news of the kingdom of God, and 72 other followers to go out even further. Today, he is still calling every Christian to proclaim the gospel, and we must be ready to give an answer to those who are willing to listen.

Sermon prompt

This sketch recognizes that we need encouragement in the difficult task of taking the good news from door to door, but it is also a warning that we need to be equipped for the job. In 1 Peter 3:15 it says, 'Always be ready to give an answer when someone asks you about your hope.' Many of us have fallen into the trap of thinking that spreading the good news is the job of those among us called to be full-time evangelists. While it is true to say that some of us will have a special gift or calling to be an evangelist, it doesn't let the rest of us off the hook. We need to have thought through some of the questions that people are likely to ask, and we must also be prepared to accommodate new people in our churches.

Cast

Two performers: KNOCKER and OPENER (both male or female).

Staging: props, costumes and effects

This sketch is set in a doorway, so you can perform it in an actual doorway (if there is one available), set up a stage door (a little more complicated) or mime the opening and closing of the door. Both characters are in everyday clothes and there are no props, but KNOCKER could carry a clipboard, as that's the sort of thing people generally take door-to-door.

Knock, knock, knocking

Scene: KNOCKER approaches a closed door. He knocks. A rather annoyed OPENER opens the door and gives KNOCKER a scowl.

Knocker: (*Cheery*) Good evening. Sorry to disturb you in your home. You don't know me but—

Opener: (*Irritated*) What do you want?

Knocker: I was just wondering… Have you ever thought about death?

Opener: Excuse me—?

Knocker: Have you ever thought about the fundamental questions of life? Who we are? Why we are here? Is there a God? Who was Jesus—?

Opener: Oh, I think you've got the wrong end of the stick here—

Knocker: And if Jesus existed… and if he did exist—was he God?

Opener: No. No. You're wasting your time. You see—

Knocker: Have you ever considered going to a church—?

Opener: If I can just stop you there. I'm already a Christian—

Knocker: Really?

Opener: Yes. And before you ask—a proper one. Baptized. Regular churchgoer. On the

Reproduced with permission from *All-age Sketches for the Christian Year* published by BRF 2006 (1 84101 458 3)

www.barnabasinchurches.org.uk

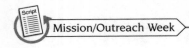

leadership team. So you'd probably be better off moving on. *(Whispering)* I've heard next door are pretty sinful...

Knocker: *(Excited)* But this is great! You're exactly the sort of person I need to talk to. You can tell me all about Jesus!

Opener: Do you mean you're not...?

Knocker: A Christian? Absolutely not! Haven't a clue. That's why I'm going door-to-door. Actually, you're the first person who hasn't slammed the door in my face—

Opener: Sounds familiar.

Knocker: So where do we start? Jesus, I suppose. He's the main one, isn't he? Tell me about him.

Opener: Oh. No. No. No. I'm not an evangelist.

Knocker: A what?

Opener: Someone whose calling is to tell people about the gospel. We did a test at cell group—

Knocker: A what group? Is it like a terrorist cell?

Opener: No, a cell group is just a small gathering of Christians during the week. Anyway, we did a test and I scored very low points as an evangelist. More likely to put people off. Best leave it to the experts.

Knocker: Can I talk to one of these experts? Could you put me in touch with your 'evangelist'?

Reproduced with permission from *All-age Sketches for the Christian Year* published by BRF 2006 (1 84101 458 3)
www.barnabasinchurches.org.uk

Opener: His name's Phil. But the problem is, his phone number doesn't always work. (THINKS) I do have an email address. But it depends on whether the satellite is aligned.

Knocker: Can't I just pop round his house?

Opener: Oh. No. He's in Togo.

Knocker: Where's that?

Opener: West Africa.

Knocker: When's he back from holiday?

Opener: Next April. It's not really a holiday. He's out there for a year evangelizing. It's amazing work. More than 30 people from this little village have given their lives to the Lord—

Knocker: Which lord?

Opener: Lord Jesus. It's a mini revival. Very exciting.

Knocker: So you can't help me then…?

Opener: I can try, I suppose. Mind you, you must have a lot of difficult questions: 'How can a God of love allow so much suffering in the world?'

Knocker: Gosh. I'd never thought of that. But you're right. How can he allow so much suffering if he's a God of love?

Opener: Tricky, isn't it? And what about evolution? And dinosaurs?

Knocker: Yeah. What about them?

www.barnabasinchurches.org.uk

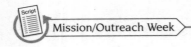

Opener: That's just the start of it. What about the Da Vinci Code? The Bible Code? (THINKS) And, um—

Knocker: The Highway Code?

Opener: Never read them, I'm afraid. Best not to meddle. Apart from the Highway Code. That's mostly safe.

Knocker: What about other religions? What's the difference between Christianity and Judaism, Islam, Buddhism, Hinduism?

Opener: Aha. Yes. I do know the answer to that. The difference—the very fundamental difference— between Christianity and all other religions is… (*Patronizing*) Christianity is the truth. And all other religions are wrong.

Knocker: But don't the other religions claim to be the truth too?

Opener: Yes. But the point, as I said, is that they are wrong and Christianity is right. You see the fundamental difference?

Knocker: Not exactly. What about Judaism? You share the same holy books partly, don't you? Are they right?

Opener: Up to a point.

Knocker: What point?

Opener: The point where they start being wrong. (BEAT) I'm making an absolute mess of this, aren't I? Sorry I can't be more helpful.

Reproduced with permission from *All-age Sketches for the Christian Year* published by BRF 2006 (1 84101 458 3)
www.barnabasinchurches.org.uk

Knocker: Isn't there a Christian book or something you can lend me?

Opener: I've got this great book about the end times.

Knocker: What's that?

Opener: Oh, it's fascinating. In Christian eschatology, the end times are a time of tribulation that will precede the second coming of Jesus. *(KNOCKER looks confused)* Maybe that's not what you need to help you become a Christian.

Knocker: But we live in a Christian country, right? Doesn't that make me a Christian?

Opener: Not at all. There's certain things you have to do.

Knocker: Such as?

Opener: Have you ever been washed in the blood of the Lamb?

Knocker: No. And I've never bathed in the spit of a yak.

Opener: Perhaps you should consider it. Not the yak spit. The Lamb's blood.

Knocker: I've had a thought! From what I remember, Jesus did miracles, didn't he? Healed people? Well, I've got this bad back. I'm in almost constant agony—

Opener: That's fantastic. Sorry, didn't mean that you being in agony is fantastic. It's just that we've started a series on healing at church.

www.barnabasinchurches.org.uk

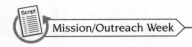

Knocker: Brilliant. Can I come along?

Opener: Unfortunately, we're only in week three. We're going through the scriptural, historical and theological basis for healing. We'll probably have a meeting where we'll pray for healing at some point. But, knowing us, it won't be for a couple of months.

Knocker: But I'm in torment... I was lifting this box at work and—

Opener: I'm really sorry, but I do have to go. I've got people over.

Knocker: Oh. Who are they?

Opener: Rather ironically, it's a group from church—

Knocker: Prayer meeting?

Opener: If only. Had no time for prayer meetings recently. It's a gathering of the finance sub-committee. We're in a rather sticky situation at the moment. The person who produced the church accounts has made a complete mess of it. And we've got to sort it out and present it to the auditors next week.

Knocker: You won't believe this! But maybe I can help you. I'm an accountant. That's what I do as a job—go in and sort out other people's financial disasters. Maybe I was meant to come here today? Shall I come in?

Opener: That's a great idea. You could come in. Help us out. I mean—we're next to useless with

Reproduced with permission from *All-age Sketches for the Christian Year* published by BRF 2006 (1 84101 458 3)
www.barnabasinchurches.org.uk

numbers. And while you're helping us, we could teach you about Jesus. There's plenty of us, so I'm sure someone will have a few answers. (BEAT) There's just one problem.

Knocker: What's that?

Opener: Church policy. To join the group... (BEAT) You have to be a Christian. Thank you for calling. Goodbye. (*Slams door*)

* * * END * * *

One rotten apple

Curtain up

Harvest Festival may seem like a throwback to the past when rural communities worked the land and relied on a bountiful harvest. Now most of us pop to the supermarket to buy our daily bread, meat, vegetables, fruit and other goods (or visit the Internet and have them delivered). It's not a very original observation, I know, but our distance from the people who sow the seed and plough the land doesn't mean they don't exist any more. The second half of September or the first week of October is traditionally the time when churches celebrate harvest, but this sketch is suitable for other agricultural festivals, too, such as Lammas, which traditionally falls at the beginning of August, and Rogationtide, which falls on the three days preceding Ascension Day.

Bible backdrop

HOSEA 12:7; AMOS 8:4–7

We can blame the supermarkets, the government or the EU and so on for not telling us enough about who is paid what percentage when we purchase our products. But ignorance is not an excuse, and neither is lack of time—not when poor people are robbed of a fair price for their daily work. God cares about justice and so should we. It's a complicated issue, where easy answers are not always the right answers, but again this does not excuse us from our personal responsibility to speak up for those who are treated unfairly to supply our daily food.

Sermon prompt

This sketch confronts the problem of fairness and aims to raise
awareness and provoke debate, rather than suggest a solution. For
each of us the answer will be different. It may require us to take a
look at where and how we do our shopping; for some it may mean
offering direct financial help to farmers; for a few it will mean taking
up the cause of the poor and educating others. If any of those things
happen as a result of this sketch, that's great.

Cast

Three performers: SUPPLY, AND and DEMAND (all male or female).

Staging: props, costumes and effects

The set for this sketch should be a market stall covered with apples.
Behind the stall is a screen large enough to prevent the audience
from seeing SUPPLY (who is on stage from the start). AND should
be dressed as a smart shopkeeper, DEMAND is in everyday clothes
and SUPPLY should look like an agricultural worker. The only props
required are some loose change and a few apples (preferably
Opalescent).

One rotten apple

Scene: A market stall covered with apples. AND is behind serving. Behind the stall is a screen where (unseen) SUPPLY is hidden. DEMAND approaches.

And: (*Humming 'We plough the fields and scatter'*) Good day to you, sir. Can I interest you in some of our delicious, affordable, life-enhancing produce?

Demand: What are you selling?

And: Only one of the best sources of quercetin and flavonoids—that's all.

Demand: Some sort of fruit?

And: To the Greeks and Romans, they were symbols of love and beauty.

Demand: Rhubarb?

And: No fruit is more elementary, more legendary, or more popular.

Demand: Kumquats?

And: It is said that if you take one of these a day, that will keep the doctor away. (*Winks*)

Demand: (*Realizes*) Oh, you mean apples!

And: Indeed I do. The humble apple. Delicious, satisfying and low in calories.

Demand: Can I buy one from you, then?

Reproduced with permission from *All-age Sketches for the Christian Year* published by BRF 2006 (1 84101 458 3)
www.barnabasinchurches.org.uk

And: Une pomme? Una manzana? Ein Apfel? Una mela? *(DEMAND looks blank)* An apple?

Demand: That's it!

And: You want to purchase the perfect portable snack? Rich in catechins, antioxidants, pectins, and vitamins A and C…?

Demand: Yeah, those. I want some.

And: Then you will have some. The customer, as they say, is always right. Now, which variety will you be partaking of?

Demand: Wot have you got?

And: Braeburns, Granny Smith, Royal Gala—

Demand: Any of those. It doesn't really matter. Apples is apples as far as I'm concerned.

And: You are truly a discerning customer. And you are right, as always. You must have a delicate yet robust palate. Able to appreciate the apple in all its colours, textures and flavours—

Demand: Got any gooseberries?

And: Your apple, sir. *(Produces apple)* One of the Opalescent variety. Would you like to try? It's a real eye-opener.

Demand: *(Takes apple)* Forbidden fruit. They call them that, too. *(Takes a small bite)* Didn't mention that in your sales patter, did you? *(Takes a bigger bite)*

And: Opalescent is one of the few early apples that are firm and juicy when fully ripe.

Demand: Very nice. Wot's the damage?

And: First one's always on the house.

Demand: There must be a catch.

And: Oh no. *(Sinister)* Not for you, sir.

Demand: *(Takes another bite)* Delicious. Yes. Go on, then. You've got me. How much for half a dozen?

And: One pound and 20 new pence.

Demand: Here you are, then. *(Pulls coin out of pocket)* One pound. *(Gives to AND)*

And: *(Examines coin and puts it in pocket)* Thank you.

Demand: And 20p.

And: *(Takes coin. Throws it over his shoulder and the screen behind. SUPPLY's arm appears from behind the screen clutching a bag of apples. AND takes them and gives them to DEMAND)* Pleasure doing business with you.

Demand: And you. *(Bites)* It's a tasty apple.

And: Right again, good customer. *(Takes out a cloth and wipes down the stall. Sings)* We plough the fields and scatter the good seed on the land…

Demand: Is that what you do, then?

And: Sir?

Demand: Plough the fields? Scatter the seed? Is that your job?

And: We don't plough the orchards, if that's what you mean—

Demand:	But you must do something. Tend to the apple trees. Pick the fruit?
And:	I'm sure, somewhere along the line, someone does the easy work.
Demand:	Easy work? What do you do, then?
And:	My role is of vital importance. Ordering, packing, advertising, marketing, selling…
Demand:	Oh, right. Well, here's a tip for ya…
And:	Yes, sir?
Demand:	These are good apples, granted. And I would have bought another bag, only—
And:	Yes?
Demand:	I passed a chap on the way here, selling a bag of six for one pound 15p.
And:	But surely, sir, ours are of a superior quality? Riper, crisper, tastier—
Demand:	I dunno about that. But I'll tell you what they're not—cheaper.
And:	If that's all that's worrying you… maybe we can come to an arrangement?
Demand:	Go on.
And:	Seeing as you, the customer, are always right, what if I were to offer you a bag of six of the finest apples for just one pound and 10 new pence?
Demand:	Now that's what I call customer relations. You're on. Another bag, please.

Reproduced with permission from *All-age Sketches for the Christian Year* published by BRF 2006 (1 84101 458 3)

www.barnabasinchurches.org.uk

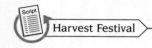

And: Any particular variety?

Demand: Don't mind at that price. *(Puts hand in pocket)* Here's the pound... *(Gives pound. AND places it in his pocket)* and 10p. *(AND takes the 10p and throws it over the screen)* You did it again. What's that all about?

And: Do you have a query about our products, sir? *(SUPPLY's hand, clutching a bag of apples, reaches out from behind the screen)*

Demand: That! *(Pointing at the hand)* There!

And: *(Grabs bag, stealthily)* Nothing you need concern yourself about, sir.

Demand: *(Takes bag of apples)* What are you hiding?

And: Do you have a problem with the quality of our produce?

Demand: Not at all.

And: Perhaps the price is too steep?

Demand: No, it's very reasonable.

And: Remember, you are always right. Why not permit yourself the bliss of—

Demand: Ignorance?

And: I was going to say 'innocence'. Don't allow yourself to be sullied by the dirty business of supply and demand.

Demand: But I'm the demand, aren't I? Is that what it is behind the screen? Your supply?

And: I prefer to think of it as the raw produce, the base goods that we—

Demand: What are you, then? If that's the supply and I'm the demand? What are you?

And: Why, I am the most important thing. The 'and'. The thing that puts the supply together with the demand. Supply and demand.

Demand: And what does your supply have to say about all this? *(Goes round the back of the screen)* Come out here. Come on. I've got a few things to ask you.

Supply: *(Sheepishly puts his head round the screen)* I'm not supposed to be seen.

Demand: Don't worry. Just a few questions. *(Shows bag)* These your apples?

Supply: No. Not mine.

And: There you are. Nothing to—

Supply: Not any more.

Demand: Why's that?

Supply: I sold them to him. So they're his now. Unless he sold them on.

Demand: How much did you sell them for?

Supply: The prices are falling all the time. I was getting 20p for half a dozen a few minutes ago. Now it's only 10p. I can't see how I'll make ends meet—

Demand: (*To AND*) But you're getting a pound a pop for these apples.

And: It's not about who's getting what, is it?

Demand: That's easy for you to say. What's to stop me from buying them from him? How does a pound sound?

Supply: Sounds very good—

And: Oh, and are you going to buy all his apples?

Demand: Well, no.

And: Then that doesn't solve the problem. I'm here to find people, drum up demand. Then put the supply with the demand.

Demand: Well, I demand that you pay him a fair price. Fair for you, and fair for him. Fair's fair.

Supply: That sounds more... fair. Don't you think?

And: I don't see why I—

Demand: What am I?

And: Well, you're a... customer.

Demand: And what are customers? Always...?

And: Right?

Demand: Right.

Supply: Right!

Demand: Why don't we go off and have a chat about this. The three of us. Work things out fairly. Listen to your customer.

And: (*Wearily*) I suppose you're... right.

Demand: What's the matter? You're not looking very well.

Supply: I've got something that may help. Just have one of these a day… (*Gives apple*)

* * * END * * *

Reproduced with permission from *All-age Sketches for the Christian Year* published by BRF 2006 (1 84101 458 3)

www.barnabasinchurches.org.uk

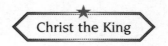

Be the centre

Curtain up

The observation of the feast of Christ the King falls on the Sunday before Advent and celebrates the kingship of Jesus, both in anticipation of his birth and in expectation of his second coming. The feast of Christ the King takes place between 20 and 26 November, depending on the date of the first Sunday of Advent.

Bible backdrop

COLOSSIANS 3:1–10

Jesus, the king of heaven, who rules at God's right side, has set out his code for living, which gives meaning and purpose to our lives. Part of being a Christian is that we become more Christ-like—more and more like our Creator. That's a pretty high target to reach!

Sermon prompt

Getting the balance right between setting our hearts on heaven and living in this world is difficult. This sketch shows an extreme example of a group of people who want to love and honour their king but don't really want to do what he says. This is therefore a sketch about where Christ is king in different areas of our lives. What do we hold back, what do we excuse, and what do we ignore? And do we really want Christ to rule in every area?

Cast

Four performers: LEADER, ONE and TWO (all male or female), who are a group of councillors; KING (male) is a representation of Jesus, but not specifically him. The sketch is a story to help us understand part of Jesus' character.

Staging: props, costumes and effects

The three councillors should be dressed smartly (suits or formal clothes). The KING should be attired in some fine regalia, topped off with a crown, so make as much effort as you can with his costume to help the audience understand his status.

The stage is just a board meeting type of set-up: a big table with four chairs for the three councillors and KING. As the cast are seated for most of the sketch, make sure they are suitably animated so as not to let the action get too static.

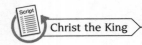

Be the centre

Scene: A council meeting. LEADER, ONE and TWO are sitting round a table. KING is sitting at the head in full regalia.

Leader: Greetings, fellow councillors. We have an unexpected special guest at our meeting today. Our great and mighty king is here. *(Indicates)* The one whom we all serve. Glorious. Magnificent. Yet kind, gracious. Wise and wonderful. Would any of you here like to take this unique opportunity to pay your respects to our beloved leader?

One: I would. I'd like to thank you, Your Majesty, for your wisdom. You alone have the answers. You have the insight, the foresight, the knowledge. There is not a problem that you cannot solve. No hidden truth that you cannot uncover. You are wise in all things. Oh that I had the words to express how much we as a body respect and value your unquestionable truth. Thank you.

Two: I should also like to say a few words, if I may. But my thanks are for your kindness, your humility, and your heart for those less fortunate. Your love for the poor among us, whether those be the poor in spirit, in heart; the poor in wisdom, or simply those unfortunate souls stricken in poverty. Your heart is ever for those people. A shining example to us all. We bow to you in gratitude.

Reproduced with permission from *All-age Sketches for the Christian Year* published by BRF 2006 (1 84101 458 3)
www.barnabasinchurches.org.uk

Leader: And I would like to add my humble voice to those who have already spoken. Your wisdom is rightly celebrated, and your heart for the poor justifiably honoured here. But I wish to offer my praise for your decrees, your laws that stem from your wisdom and heart. They are sacred to us all. Thank you for your many insights into how we should live our lives. Thank you that your laws are fair and just. Thank you that they are a blessing to us all. But most of all, we thank you that we have been honoured with the task of communicating and representing these great decrees. Thank you that it is up to us to rule over this land of yours. And thank you that you have willingly given us the task to do this.

King: And thank you all for your kind words. I am happy just to be here with you.

Leader: If you don't mind, great king, we are about to perform our duties. We have been honoured by your presence. Now you may leave. Goodbye. *(Indicates for KING to go)*

One: Goodbye.

Two: Goodbye.

King: I thought I might stay for the meeting.

Leader: Oh.

King: If that's OK?

Leader: Oh, absolutely.

Reproduced with permission from *All-age Sketches for the Christian Year* published by BRF 2006 (1 84101 458 3)

www.barnabasinchurches.org.uk

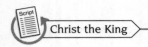
One:	Great.
Two:	Wonderful.
Leader:	We have but a few trifling matters to attend to. It won't be of great interest to one so mighty—
King:	I'm sure it will be of interest.
One:	Not really—
Two:	A lot of fiddling details we have to get through—
Leader:	Nothing for you to concern yourself with—
One:	I'm sure you have some more highbrow—
Two:	Kingly things to bother with—
Leader:	Haven't you?
King:	Everything in my kingdom is important to me.
Leader:	Great. Let's have the meeting as usual. What's on the agenda for today?
One:	First topic: stealing. Unlawfully taking things that are not yours.
Two:	Stealing is wrong. That's my first thought.
Leader:	I think we all agree on that.
One:	Absolutely. Stealing big, noticeable things is very wrong.
Two:	Inexcusable.
Leader:	That's why we have laws.

PAUSE.

Reproduced with permission from *All-age Sketches for the Christian Year* published by BRF 2006 (1 84101 458 3)
www.barnabasinchurches.org.uk

One:	What about smaller things?
Two:	Things people don't really miss…
Leader:	… or deserve.
One:	I think it's OK to steal those sorts of things, within reason.
Two:	Like taking a bigger slice of cake.
Leader:	Or withholding things from people.
One:	Keeping things for oneself, for example.
Two:	Nothing wrong with that, is there?
Leader:	No.
One:	Of course not.
King:	Can I say something?
Leader:	Why, yes, great king.
King:	It is our duty to treat others better than ourselves. So we should make sure that others are given a greater share than we have. I want you to be generous, not to hoard things up for yourselves.
One:	Thank you, we will take that into consideration. (PAUSE) So, we're agreed. Stealing, under certain circumstances, is OK.
Leader:	Exactly. Businesses stealing from people is OK, for example. Surely?
Two:	Yes. In the same way, borrowing a bit of stationery from a business is fine. Who's going to notice? Or doing personal things in company time is OK, within reason.

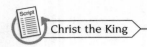

One: So long as you don't take the mick.

Two: Or get caught! (*All except KING laugh*)

King: Haven't you been listening?

Leader: Stealing is wrong. We know that. Absolutely.

One: Wrong. Wrong. Wrong.

Two: In principle.

Leader: But in the day-to-day, run-of-the-mill course of events—

One: Sometimes it's unavoidable.

Two: So what's the point of making a big fuss—?

Leader: Not of the little things.

One: Makes criminals out of people.

Two: Look at it this way. Sometimes you're in a rush to catch a train…

Leader: No time to get a ticket…

One: It's not like they check…

Two: And, by then, you've already been on the journey…

Leader: You could find a machine and buy a ticket…

One: But who would know?

Two: It's a victimless crime.

Leader: Or like when you check your receipt and find they haven't charged you for something…

One: Or you find you've got a little extra in your pay packet. Might just be an oversight.

Reproduced with permission from *All-age Sketches for the Christian Year* published by BRF 2006 (1 84101 458 3)
www.barnabasinchurches.org.uk

Two: No point in checking.

Leader: Little unauthorized bonus. No one needs to know…

King: And where does that leave the law?

Leader: We respect your laws.

One: We honour your laws.

Two: We welcome your laws.

Leader: But sometimes we must adapt your laws. We need a way to work them out in everyday circumstances. Take the second item on the agenda: lying.

King: I would hope that my people would strive to be open and honest and have integrity in what they say and do.

One: Of course, we understand that lying is wrong.

Two: It's deceitful.

Leader: Unhelpful.

One: Hurtful.

Two: But sometimes it's necessary.

Leader: We wish it wasn't.

One: We wish it was possible not to lie.

Two: But sometimes you have to.

Leader: Sometimes you're forced to.

One: Sometimes it's easier.

Two: Sometimes it's for the best.

Reproduced with permission from *All-age Sketches for the Christian Year* published by BRF 2006 (1 84101 458 3)

www.barnabasinchurches.org.uk

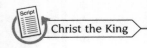

Leader: Even if it's wrong.

King: I don't understand. You say I am your king?

One: Of course, Great One.

Two: Why, yes, Your Magnificence.

Leader: Absolutely, Your Highness.

King: Then you should strive to do what I have said. Yearn to live by my standards. Love to obey my laws.

One: I'm very sorry, Your Excellence. But, if you don't mind me saying, these meetings were an awful lot easier when you weren't here among us.

Two: This whole black-and-white thing—it's not really 'now'.

Leader: People don't think like that any more.

One: If they ever did.

Two: And while we welcome your laws as a starting point...

Leader: It's up to us to deal with the details...

One: Work things out in practical terms...

Two: Maybe it would be easier if you left it up to us.

Leader: It's very nice that you came here.

One: Put on the regalia.

Two: Wore the crown.

Leader: But we think it would be better if you left.

Reproduced with permission from *All-age Sketches for the Christian Year* published by BRF 2006 (1 84101 458 3)
www.barnabasinchurches.org.uk

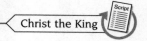

King: Do you still want me to be king?

One: Oh, absolutely.

Two: Couldn't do without you.

Leader: We just prefer you to do it somewhere else, that's all.

* * * END * * *

Index of Bible references

★ Also from Barnabas ★

The Gospels Unplugged

52 poems and stories for creative writing, RE, drama and collective worship

Lucy Moore

This book is for busy church leaders who have endless demands on their time and energy and need stories that jump off the page, into the imagination and, from there, into daily life. Drawn from all four Gospels, the pieces are 'unplugged' in that they get to the heart of the biblical text, reflecting the life of Jesus in action: who he is, what he said and what he did. Some tell the story; some explore an aspect of the original account.

Each piece comes with a short introduction of open-ended questions to encourage further exploration of the original story and the relevant Bible passage for reference. Some pieces are meant to be performed, some to be enjoyed quietly; but the overall aim is to have fun and enjoy unplugging the Gospels!

ISBN 1 84101 243 2   £12.99
Available from your local Christian bookshop or, in case of difficulty, direct from BRF using the order form on page 189.

Launchpad

17 child-centred service outlines for all-age worship

Neil Pugmire and Mark Rodel

This book contains all you need to create child-centred, adult-friendly services for your church. With five series to choose from and 17 service frameworks in total, *Launchpad* is designed to 'launch' children from the age of five into the Christian faith by presenting the gospel in a clear, exciting and non-patronizing way, while at the same time communicating profound truths to enable adult members of the congregation to discover new things about God.

Topics include meeting God's heroes, living in harmony, the story of David, the events of Holy Week and Easter, and an Advent series based on the gifts of the magi. Alongside the 17 service frameworks, there is a comprehensive introduction giving lots of advice to get you started.

Each service framework includes:

- Clear teaching points and talk outlines
- References for Bible passages, plus key verses in full
- Full drama script with photocopy permission
- Suggested songs from published resources
- Prayers

ISBN 1 84101 326 9   £7.99
Available from your local Christian bookshop or, in case of difficulty, direct from BRF using the order form on page 189.

ORDER FORM

REF	TITLE	PRICE	QTY	TOTAL
243 2	*The Gospels Unplugged*	£12.99		
326 9	*Launchpad*	£7.99		

POSTAGE AND PACKING CHARGES					Postage and packing:	
Order value	UK	Europe	Surface	Air Mail	Donation:	
£7.00 & under	£1.25	£3.00	£3.50	£5.50	**Total enclosed:**	
£7.01–£30.00	£2.25	£5.50	£6.50	£10.00		
Over £30.00	free	prices on request				

Name _____ Account Number _____

Address_____

_____ Postcode _____

Telephone Number _____ Email _____

Payment by: ❏ Cheque ❏ Mastercard ❏ Visa ❏ Postal Order ❏ Switch

Card no. ❏❏❏❏ ❏❏❏❏ ❏❏❏❏ ❏❏❏❏

Expires ❏❏ ❏❏   Issue no. of Switch card ❏❏❏

Signature _____ Date _____

All orders must be accompanied by the appropriate payment.

Please send your completed order form to:
BRF, First Floor, Elsfield Hall, 15–17 Elsfield Way, Oxford OX2 8FG
Tel. 01865 319700 / Fax. 01865 319701 Email: enquiries@brf.org.uk

❏ Please send me further information about BRF publications.

Available from your local Christian bookshop.   BRF is a Registered Charity

Resourcing people to work with 3–11s

in churches and schools

- Articles, features, ideas
- Training and events
- Books and resources
- www.barnabasinchurches.org.uk

Barnabas is an imprint of brf

BRF is a Registered Charity